Unterrichtsmodell

Series Editor: Hans Kröger

Aldous Huxley
Brave New World

by Angela Luz and
Brigitte Prischtt

Best.-Nr. 041249 5

Schöningh

EINFACH ENGLISCH

- Arbeitsfrage
- filmische Präsentation
- Einzelarbeit
- Partnerarbeit
- Gruppenarbeit
- Unterrichtsgespräch
- Schreibauftrag
- Hausaufgabe
- Projektorientierung, offenes Unterrichtsangebot
- Aufgaben mit kreativem Ansatz
- Szenisches Spiel, Rollenspiel

Vorwort

Der Titel der Reihe **EinFach Englisch** ist Ziel und Programm zugleich. Einerseits sollen Schülerinnen und Schülern literarische Zusammenhänge erklärt und ihnen damit der Zugang zu klassischen, aber auch neueren literarischen Werken erleichtert werden, und dies soll auf sprachlich einfache Art und Weise erfolgen, wodurch man der heutigen Schülergeneration sicherlich eher gerecht werden kann als mit schwierigen und komplexen Ansätzen. Andererseits sollen Lehrkräften erprobte und aus der Praxis stammende Unterrichtsmodelle angeboten werden, die ihnen einen raschen Zugriff auf unterschiedliche Materialien ermöglichen und einen Leitfaden für die Behandlung fiktionaler Texte oder die Analyse von Filmen im Unterricht bieten. Die Modelle können direkt und ohne Umschweife eingesetzt werden, langes Einlesen und eine zeitintensive Beschäftigung mit dem Stoff sind nicht erforderlich, wodurch die Arbeit, insbesondere die Unterrichtsvorbereitung von Lehrerinnen und Lehrern, erheblich erleichtert werden kann.
Schnell erhält man einen Überblick über **Figurenkonstellation** und **Inhalt** und kann sich problemlos entscheiden, ob ein Werk für eine bestimmte Reihe geeignet ist. Man weiß vorab, welche **Klausur** mit welchen Schwerpunkten geschrieben werden kann, und kann dieses bei der konkreten Planung eines Kursabschnittes entsprechend berücksichtigen. **Arbeitsblätter** sind als Kopiervorlagen gestaltet und **Tafelbilder** sind eingebettet in die **Leitfragen** zum eigentlichen Unterrichtsgeschehen, d. h., Material, das eingesetzt werden soll, befindet sich dort, wo es gebraucht wird; langes Suchen entfällt. **Piktogramme** geben optische Hilfen und Hinweise, sodass leicht zu erkennen ist, welche **Sozial-** bzw. **Arbeitsformen** sich bei den jeweiligen Aufgaben anbieten.
Die Unterrichtsmodelle basieren auf bewährten Verfahren der Textinterpretation und der Filmanalyse, dabei fließen neuere Erkenntnisse und Ansätze zu einer modernen Textrezeption angemessen ein. Der Umfang des Materials ist auf die tatsächlichen Gegebenheiten der Unterrichtspraxis abgestimmt und es sollte möglich sein, das Unterrichtsmodell vollständig und nicht nur in Auszügen im Rahmen einer Unterrichtsreihe einzusetzen. Das Prinzip der **„Components"** ermöglicht es darüber hinaus den Benutzern, unterschiedliche Reihen zu konzipieren, die an unterschiedlichen thematischen Schwerpunkten oder methodischen Fertigkeiten orientiert sind und ganz den individuellen oder kursspezifischen Bedürfnissen angepasst werden können. Dabei erheben die Unterrichtsmodelle nicht den Anspruch der Vollständigkeit, sondern eher den der Machbarkeit und Praxisnähe.

Das vorliegende Modell bezieht sich auf folgende Textausgabe:
Aldous Huxley, *Brave New World*, Reclam, Ditzingen 1998,
ISBN: 3-15-009284-1

Sprachliche Betreuung: Simone Duxbury-Ziemer

www.schoeningh.de
Schöningh Verlag, Jühenplatz 1–3, 33098 Paderborn

Druck A 5 4 3 2 1 / Jahr 2009 08 07 06 05
Alle Drucke der Serie A sind im Unterricht parallel verwendbar.
Die letzte Zahl bezeichnet das Jahr dieses Druckes.

Druck und Bindung: AZ Druck und Datentechnik GmbH/Kempten (Allgäu)

ISBN 3-14-041249-5

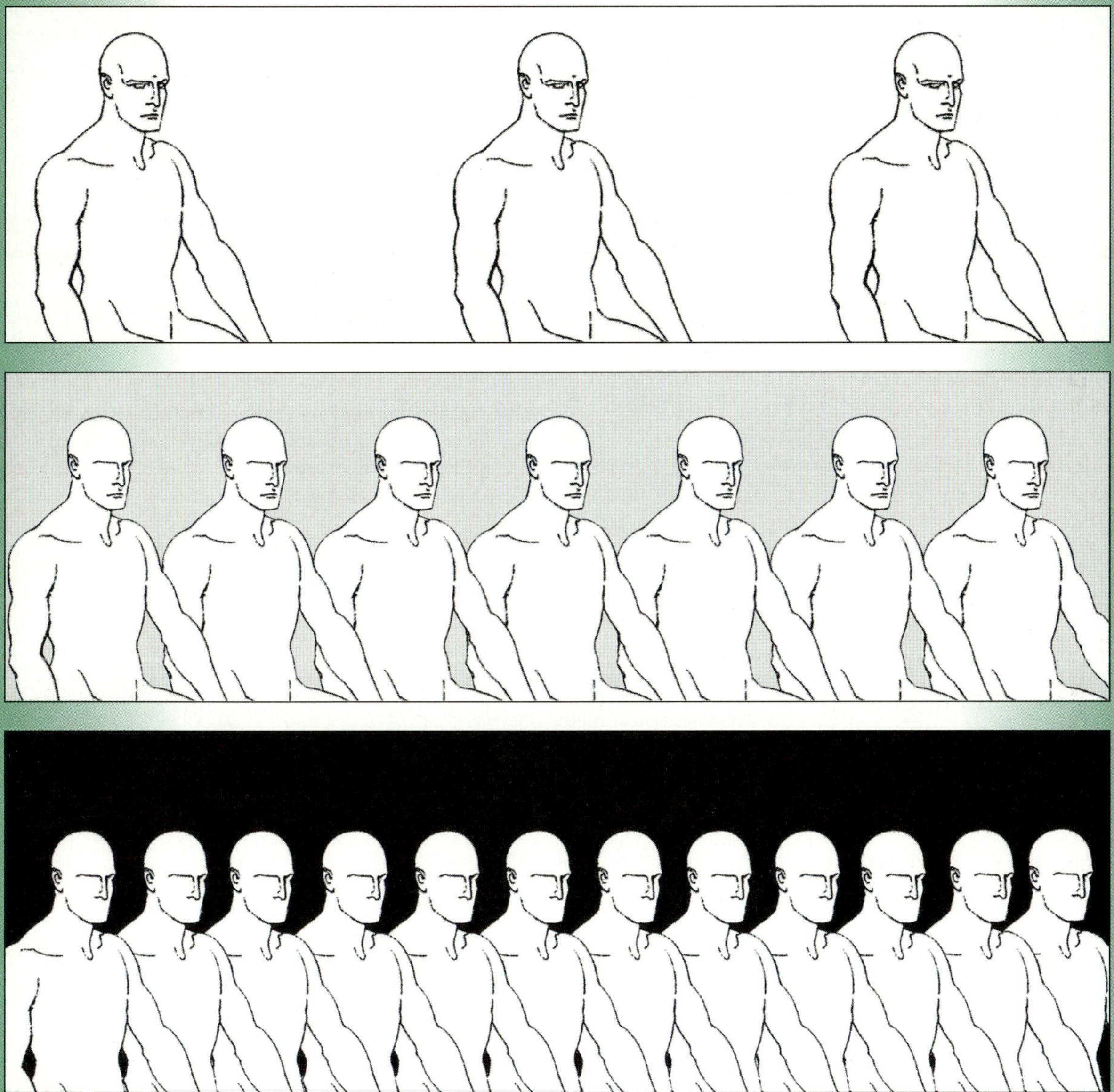

Grafik: Victor Prischtt

Components

Aldous Huxley: *Brave New World*

Component 1
Understanding the Novel

worksheets 1–9

Component 2
Brave New World – a Dystopian Novel of the 30's

2.1 Dystopia	Kopiervorlage
2.2 Let's talk to the experts	Kopiervorlagen/worksheet 10

Component 3
Behavioural Engineering

3.1 Classical conditioning	Kopiervorlage
3.2 Behaviourism	Kopiervorlage
3.3 Hypnopaedia	Kopiervorlage/worksheets 11a, 11b/Szenenübersicht (Film)

Component 4
Community, Identity, Stability

4.1 The use of drugs	worksheet 12
4.2 Cultural life	
4.3 The role of the media	

Component 5
Wrapping up the Novel

worksheets 13a–15

Contents

Die Personen

Mustapha Mond Einer der zehn Weltkontrolleure, die den Weltstaat regieren. Er ist ein intelligenter Kenner Shakespeares, der Bibel, der Geschichte und der Philosophie, der sich als junger, begabter Wissenschaftler einst bewusst gegen die Rolle des Dissidenten und für eine Karriere als Herrscher der Welt entschied.

Der Direktor Leiter des Londoner Brut- und Konditionierungszentrums, ein Alpha, der sich in seiner Position als Leiter sehr wichtig nimmt und dies den Studenten gegenüber sehr betont. Er ist ein vollkommener Konformist. Allerdings beging er vor vielen Jahren den Fehler, seine schwangere Geliebte in einem Reservat der „wilden" Welt zurückgelassen zu haben. Als John, ihrer beider Sohn, in London auftaucht und sich zu erkennen gibt, ist er zutiefst gedemütigt, gesellschaftlich ruiniert und am Ende seiner Karriere.

Helmholtz Watson Er stellt den perfekten Alpha dar: gut aussehend, stark, intelligent und erfolgreich in Beruf, Sport und bei den Frauen. Er liebt die Sprache und schreibt Propaganda für den Weltstaat, ist sich jedoch auch bewusst, dass er zu Höherem fähig ist, als der Staat zulässt. Er ist den Außenseitern der Gesellschaft, John und Bernard, ein guter Freund und wird am Ende auf die Falkland Inseln verbannt. Im Gegensatz zu Bernard sieht er in der Abgeschiedenheit der Inseln und der Gesellschaft von anderen Dissidenten aber die Chance, zum Schreiben inspiriert zu werden.

Henry Foster Er vertritt den typischen Bürger des Weltstaates: Wissenschaftler im Londoner Brut- und Konditionierungszentrum, sehr effizient und pünktlich in seiner Arbeit. Seine Freizeit verbringt er planmäßig und sittenkonform mit Sport und unverbindlichem Sex mit häufig wechselnden Frauen. Allerdings hat er eine längere Beziehung zu Lenina, die sich am Ende des Romans jedoch auch als sehr oberflächlich erweist, lässt er sie doch im Stich, als sie angegriffen wird.

Bernard Marx Er ist der Spezialist für Hypnopädie (eine Methode, durch die Menschen mit wiederholten Sprüchen während des Schlafens indoktriniert werden), der zu der Gruppe der intelligenten Alphas gehört. Allerdings wird er wegen seiner geringen Größe als hässlich und deformiert angesehen. Man vermutet, dass seine Entwicklung gestört wurde, als ihm als Embryo versehentlich eine falsche Dosis Alkohol verabreicht wurde. Die Zugabe von Alkohol dient im Weltstaat der Schaffung von Babys geringerer Qualität für die unteren sozialen Gruppen. Er leidet deswegen unter einem Minderwertigkeitskomplex und weicht insofern von der Norm ab, als er keinen Sport treibt und gern allein ist. Er fliegt mit Lenina ins Indianerreservat und entdeckt dort John, bringt ihn nach London und wird so für die Gesellschaft wichtig. Die Wissenschaftler interessieren sich für ihn und auch die Frauen scheinen ihn plötzlich attraktiv zu finden. Er genießt diese neue Stellung und scheint all seine Kritik an der Gesellschaft zu vergessen. Am Ende des Romans, nachdem es ihm nicht gelingt, John auf einer Party zu präsentieren, wird er nach Island verbannt.

Lenina Crowne Eine fast perfekt gelungene Weltstaatenbürgerin: Hübsch, oberflächlich und glücklich amüsiert sie sich beim Freizeitsport, bei *feelies* (Fühlkino) und mit wechselnden Liebhabern. Sie hinterfragt die Prinzipien der Gesellschaft nicht, verstößt aber gegen die „guten Sitten", indem sie eine inakzeptabel lange monogame Beziehung zu Henry Foster pflegt, Mitleid für Bernard Marx empfindet und sich für die altmodischen Vorstellungen Johns interessiert (allerdings unfähig, sie begreifen zu können), sich sogar in ihn verliebt.

Linda Linda ist eine Beta, die 25 Jahre vor dem Einsetzen der Romanhandlung nach einem Urlaub im Indianerreservat schwanger von dem späteren Direktor zurückgelassen wird, da er sie nach einem Unfall für tot hält. So fristet sie ein Außenseiterdasein im Reservat, von den Indianern wegen ihrer lockeren Moralvorstellungen nicht akzeptiert. Sie versteht nicht, warum ihre Lebensweise auf Ablehnung stößt, und versucht durch übermäßigen Drogen- und Alkoholkonsum sowie einen Liebhaber ihr Leben erträglicher zu gestalten. Als sie durch den Besuch von Bernard und Lenina wieder in ihre alte perfekte Welt zurückkommt, ist diese geschockt angesichts der aufgrund mangelnder medizinischer Versorgung und einfachen Lebens sichtbar gealterten, kranken, übergewichtigen, ungepflegten Frau, die skandalöserweise ein Kind (John) auf natürliche Weise zur Welt gebracht hat. Verachtet sowohl von den Indianern als auch von den Weltstaatbewohnern sucht sie Zuflucht in der glücksbringenden Droge *Soma* und stirbt bald.

John, the Savage Er ist der Sohn von Linda und dem Direktor, der ohne seinen Vater im Indianerreservat aufwächst. Er wird geprägt von drei Kulturen: der der Indianer voller Mythen und strengen religiösen und moralischen Vorstellungen, der seiner Mutter, die ihm immer wieder von dem lockeren, sorgenfreien Leben im Weltstaat erzählt, und der der Wertvorstellungen, die er durch die intensive Lektüre von Shakespeares Werken erfährt. Als Lenina und Bernard im Reservat auftauchen und sich die Gelegenheit bietet, sie nach London zu begleiten, ist John sehr begierig, diese *„Brave New World"* kennen zu lernen. Bald schon stellt sich heraus, dass die oberflächliche Spaß- und Konsumgesellschaft seinen Wertvorstellungen nicht entspricht. Seine kulturelle Prägung macht es ihm unmöglich, eine Beziehung zu Lenina einzugehen. Er verliebt sich zwar in sie, wird aber von ihrem lockeren Umgang mit Sex abgestoßen. So muss er am Ende des Romans zutiefst enttäuscht erkennen, dass auch in der Welt seiner Mutter kein Platz für ihn ist. Angewidert von der Gesellschaft, von der ihm seine Mutter in der Außenseitersituation im Reservat immer vorgeschwärmt hatte, sieht er im Freitod den einzigen Ausweg für sich.

Der Inhalt

Brave New World spielt in London im Jahre 2540, 632 Jahre nach dem Erscheinen von Fords berühmtem T-Modell. Die Welt ist ein einziger Weltstaat, in dem alles (die Menschen eingeschlossen) perfekt geplant und hierarchisch durchorganisiert ist. Babys werden nach Bedarf der Gesellschaft bestellt und wachsen nach künstlicher Befruchtung in Flaschen. Sie werden physisch und psychologisch konditioniert, um sie zu glücklichen und nützlichen Mitgliedern der Gesellschaft zu machen. Die Gesellschaft ist in fünf Klassen eingeteilt, von den intelligenten *Alphas* bis zu den *Epsilons,* die einfache Arbeiten erledigen. Zehn *controller* regieren diesen Weltstaat, der von Wohlstand, Problemfreiheit, Spaß und Konsum gekennzeichnet ist und auf dem Prinzip *„no leisure from pleasure"* basiert. Ausgenommen von dieser totalen Ordnung der Welt sind nur einige Reservate, in denen die Eingeborenen noch so leben wie zu Henry Fords Zeiten.

Zu Beginn des Romans führt der Direktor eine Gruppe von Studenten durch das *Central London Hatchery and Conditioning Centre* und erklärt, wie die Babys entstehen und wie ihre Gefühle und Einstellungen durch Konditionierung und Hypnopädie auf die Erfordernisse der Gesellschaft eingestellt werden. Mustapha Mond, der für Westeuropa zuständige *controller,* erläutert die Gründe für die Schaffung dieser voll kontrollierten Gesellschaft. Ein weiterer Alpha, Henry Foster, Assistent des Direktors, wohnt der Führung auch bei und sie stoßen auf Lenina Crowne, eine von Henry Fosters Geliebten und Krankenschwester im Brutzentrum. Lenina wird von ihrer Freundin Fanny wegen ihrer langen Beziehung zu Henry kritisiert. Sie verstößt damit gegen die Regeln der emotionslosen Spaßgesellschaft, für die Promiskuität wichtig ist.

So kommt sie mit Bernard Marx zusammen, einem um gesellschaftliche Anerkennung ringenden Alpha, der sehr klein geraten ist und der Gesellschaft sehr kritisch gegenübersteht. Die beiden verbringen ihren Urlaub in einem Reservat in New Mexico, wo die Eingeborenen wie „Wilde" leben. Überraschenderweise treffen sie dort auf John, einen jungen Weißen, der Englisch spricht und Shakespeare zitiert. Es stellt sich heraus, dass seine Mutter Linda 25 Jahre zuvor dort von dem Direktor nach einem Unfall schwanger zurückgelassen wurde und seitdem schwer mit ihrem Schicksal hadert. Unfähig, sich in ihre neue Umgebung integrieren zu können, fristet sie ein unglückliches Außenseiterdasein und versucht sich mit Alkohol und Drogen zu trösten.

Linda und John, *„the Savage"*, begleiten Lenina und Bernard nach London, wo Linda sich ganz dem so lange vermissten Genuss von *Soma,* der üblichen Droge im Weltstaat, hingibt. John, der mit den Mythen der Indianer und den Moralvorstellungen aus Shakespeares Werken aufgewachsen ist, ist so entsetzt von dieser von ihm mit einem Shakespeare-Zitat aus *The Tempest* als *„Brave New World"* bezeichneten Welt und ihren so konträren Werten, dass er sich weigert, eine zu seinen Ehren veranstalte Party zu besuchen, durch die Bernard gesellschaftlich avancieren wollte. Desillusioniert tauscht Bernard seine gesellschaftskritischen Gedanken mit Helmholtz Watson aus, der sein Sprachvermögen dazu nutzt, für den Weltstaat Propaganda zu schreiben, jedoch auch die Poesie liebt und von Johns Shakespeare-Zitaten beeindruckt ist.

Lenina fühlt sich zu John hingezogen und nähert sich ihm auf ihre „moderne“ Art, wodurch sie seine Verachtung provoziert, obwohl er sich in sie verliebt hat.

Als John am Sterbebett seiner Mutter sitzt, muss er erkennen, dass niemand seine Trauer nachvollziehen kann. In der Spaßgesellschaft sind tiefe Gefühle und innige menschliche Bindungen wegkonditioniert worden. Völlig aufgewühlt versucht John die einfachen Arbeiter des Krankenhauses von dieser Konditionierung zu befreien, indem er die übliche Ausgabe der beruhigenden Droge *Soma* zu verhindern sucht. Die erbosten Arbeiter können nur durch die Polizei (und Ausgabe der Droge) besänftigt werden. John und die ihm zu Hilfe gekommenen Bernard und Helmholtz werden dem *controller* vorgeführt, der ihnen die Wichtigkeit der *social stability* für die Gesellschaft vor Augen hält, in der kein Raum ist für Kunst, Religion oder Wissenschaft. Bernard und Helmholtz werden auf entlegene Inseln verbannt, während John sich vollkommen aus der Gesellschaft zurückzieht.
Er findet Zuflucht in einem einsam gelegenen verlassenen Leuchtturm, wo er als Einsiedler auch Selbstzüchtigung für seine Sünden praktiziert. Dadurch wird er für die Presse interessant, die wiederum viele Zuschauer anlockt, die John leiden sehen wollen. Als John Lenina unter den Schaulustigen entdeckt, erhängt er sich.

The Author

Aldous Leonard Huxley was born as the youngest of three sons on July 26, 1894 in Surrey, England. The members of his family belonged to the English intellectual elite and had become famous for their contribution to science and literature. Among them were his grandfather, Thomas Henry Huxley, a great biologist who helped develop Darwin's theory of evolution, along with famous novelists, poets, literary critics and educators. His father was a successful teacher, editor and author, and his mother was also a very well-educated woman.

Aldous Huxley followed the normal path of children of the English upper-middle class and in 1908 started at the prestigious Eton college. In the same year his beloved mother died of cancer. When he was 16, an eye illness made him nearly blind shortly before he was to finish school. Despite this he continued his studies by learning Braille, and in 1913, he was able to start his studies at Oxford. Originally, he had intended to study medicine, but due to his eye disease he instead began a degree in English literature in 1916 – the same year he also published his first book: a collection of poems. He never lost his interest in scientific ideas, though, and incorporated them in his books, especially in *Brave New World.* His near-blindness also prevented him from enlisting in World War I in 1914, the same year his brother Trevenen committed suicide on account of unrequited love.

In 1919, Huxley married Maria Nys, a Belgian, and in 1920, their only child, a daughter was born. In the following years, he established himself as a novelist and essayist, and the family began to travel, spending a lot of time in Italy and Southern France. In 1925 and 1926, they travelled around the world, also visiting India and the USA.

Before writing *Brave New World* in 1931, Huxley had published various stories, essays, poems and plays, including his bestseller *Point Counter Point* (1927).
In 1937, the family settled in California and Huxley became a screenwriter for Hollywood movies (e.g. an adaptation of Jane Austen's *Pride and Prejudice* with Laurence Olivier). In 1946, after the experience of World War II, Huxley wrote the foreword to *Brave New World,* in which he affirmed that he did not want to make social sanity an impossibility any longer in the way that he had done in the novel. Yet he always thought about the dangers that threatened the sanity of society. He published these thoughts in 1958 in *Brave New World Revisited,* a collection of essays on real-life problems that are present in the novel (e.g. overpopulation, overorganization, and psychological techniques such as propaganda, the art of selling, brainwashing and hypnopaedia).

Huxley's interest in mind-expanding drugs led him to take mescaline and LSD under supervision at various times. He wrote about these experiences in *The Doors of Perception* (1954) and *Heaven and Hell* (1956). The title of the first book gave name to Jim Morrison's band *The Doors.*

By the time Aldous Huxley died of cancer in 1963 in his home in Hollywood, he had published 47 books (both novels and essays). The most famous are: *Crome Yellow (1921), Antic Hay (1923), Point Counter Point (1928), Brave New World (1931), After Many a Summer Dies the Swan (1939),* and *Island (1962),* a utopian novel that stands in contrast to the dystopia described in *Brave New World.*

In 1971, his ashes were returned to England and interred in his parents' grave in Surrey.

Vorüberlegungen zum Einsatz des Romans im Unterricht

Huxleys Roman *Brave New World,* der seinen Platz im Lektürekanon der Oberstufe in den Fächern Englisch und Deutsch seit langer Zeit behauptet hat, hat in den letzten Jahren aufgrund der rasanten Weiterentwicklung der Gentechnologie eine vom Autor nicht vorhersehbare Aktualität erreicht. Thematisch lässt sich die Lektüre dieses Romans an unterschiedliche Themenbereiche anknüpfen, so selbstverständlich in den Bereich *Utopia/Dystopia,* der beispielsweise in den Empfehlungen für den Lektüreunterricht in NRW im Hinblick auf das Zentralabitur festgeschrieben ist. Darüber hinaus kann man ihn bei der Bearbeitung der Themen *Media, Drugs* und *Our Future* einsetzen.

Die Lektüre des Romans zwingt die Leser zur Auseinandersetzung mit den Fragen, inwieweit alltägliche Einrichtungen in unserer Gesellschaft auf dem Hintergrund der überspitzten Darstellung in *Brave New World* neu betrachtet werden müssen. Man kann sich nicht über die massenhafte Einnahme von *Soma* durch alle Bewohner der schönen neuen Welt wundern, ohne gleichzeitig darüber nachzudenken, wie unreflektiert in unserer Gesellschaft legale und illegale Drogen und Psychopharmaka konsumiert werden, um dieselben Ziele zu erreichen. Ähnliche Überlegungen bieten sich bei der Besprechung von *Feelies, Hypnopaedia* und anderen auf den ersten Blick merkwürdigen Einrichtungen an, wodurch die Schülerinnen und Schüler angeregt werden können, über ihren Medienkonsum nachzudenken. Diese Arbeit wird unterstützt durch ein Zitat von Neil Postman und Gesprächsanregungen zu den Themen Ritalin, Prozac und Medienkritik.

Die Bearbeitung der *Components 2–5* sollte auf der Grundlage der abgeschlossenen Lektüre des Romans erfolgen. Ein Problem bei der Vorablektüre besteht darin, dass man sich nicht sicher sein kann, dass alle Kursteilnehmer den Roman auch wirklich gelesen haben. Daher bietet *Component 1* eine Sammlung von *Worksheets,* die für jedes Kapitel Aufgaben zur Bearbeitung bietet. Je nach Arbeitseifer und Leistungsstärke des Kurses können alle *Worksheets* an alle Teilnehmer ausgeteilt werden oder auch arbeitsteilig einzelne Schülerinnen und Schüler einzelne Kapitel mithilfe der *Worksheets* zusammenfassen und präsentieren. Die Besprechung der *Worksheets* sollte nicht geballt vor Beginn der Arbeit an den folgenden *Components* durchgeführt werden, sondern sukzessive parallel zur Arbeit an den *Components* in den Unterricht einfließen. Dabei wäre es denkbar, vor jedem *Component* zwei bis drei *Worksheets* zu bearbeiten. Da eine genaue Kenntnis für die Bearbeitung der Bausteine wichtig ist, darf diese Arbeit nicht zu wenig Raum einnehmen. Falls man die *Worksheets* nicht benutzen möchte, sollten die Kapitel kurz vorgestellt und knappe Zusammenfassungen im Kurs aufgehängt werden.

Obwohl die Verfasserinnen den Film für eine missglückte Umsetzung des Romans halten, findet sich in *Component 3* eine detaillierte Szenenfolge, die helfen soll, sich innerhalb des Films zu orientieren, falls man andere als die im Unterrichtsmodell besprochenen Szenen zur Bearbeitung heranziehen möchte.

Neben der Verfilmung von *Brave New World* (von Leslie Libman und Larry Williams, USA 1998) gibt es Audiokassetten, z.B. Harper Collins Audio Books, Aldous Huxley, *Brave New World,* read by Tony Britton (abridged).

Die dem Unterrichtsmodell zugrunde liegende Ausgabe von *Brave New World* stammt aus dem Reclam Verlag (Bestellnummer 9284).

Klausuren

Im Folgenden werden zwei Klausurvorschläge zum Roman *Brave New World* vorgestellt.

Klausur 1 besteht aus einem nicht-fiktionalen Text aus dem *Time Magazine* vom 10. März 1997, der sich mit den möglichen schrecklichen Folgen der Gentechnik beschäftigt. Es wird dargestellt, dass es Diktatoren in Zukunft möglich sein könnte, ihre Herrschaft über Klone über ihren Tod hinaus zu sichern. Diese Klausur sollte nicht vor der Bearbeitung von *Component 2* gestellt werden, da dann die Schülerinnen und Schüler sowohl den gesamten Roman gelesen als auch durch die Beschäftigung mit den fünf Texten des Expertenpuzzles bereits erfahren haben, dass es sowohl Begründungen für als auch gegen eine weitere Förderung der Gentechnik und damit eine Ausweitung der Experimente auch mit menschlichem Genmaterial gibt. Diese Klausur eignet sich besonders gut für einen Leistungskurs, da der Text anspruchsvoll ist und eine umfassende Auseinandersetzung mit dem Problem der Entwicklung von Techniken, die das Klonen von Menschen ermöglichen, erfordert.

Klausur 2 basiert auf einer Textstelle aus dem Roman: S. 150ff., Kapitel VII. In dem Textausschnitt trifft Lenina zum ersten Mal auf Linda und reagiert geschockt. Dieser Textausschnitt eignet sich auch zur Bearbeitung durch einen Grundkurs; man könnte die wahlweise gestellte Aufgabe 4 insofern kürzen, als man nur die kreative Aufgabe stellt. Voraussetzung für die Bearbeitung der Klausur ist die Beherrschung von Stilmitteln, die man allerdings in einer 12./13. Jahrgangsstufe voraussetzen können sollte.

Notizen:

Dick Thompson: "Will We Follow the Sheep?"

The despot will not be coming to the cloning lab today. Before long, he knows, the lab's science will come to him – and not a moment too soon. The despot has ruled his little country for 30 years, but now he's getting old and will have to pass on his power. That makes him nervous; he has seen what can happen to a cult of personality if too weak a personality takes over. Happily, in his country that is not a danger. As soon as the technology of the cloning lab goes global – as it inevitably must – his people can be assured of his leadership long after he is gone.

This is the ultimate nightmare scenario. The Pharaohs built their pyramids, the Emperors built Rome, and Napoleon built his Arc de Triomphe – all, at least in part, to make the permanence of stone compensate for the impermanence of the flesh. But big buildings and big tombs would be a poor second choice if the flesh could be made to go on forever. Now, it appears, it can.

The idea of a dictator's being genetically duplicated is not new – not in pop culture, anyhow. In Ira Levin's 1976 book *The Boys from Brazil*, a zealous ex-Nazi bred a generation of literal Hitler Youth – boys cloned from cells left behind by the Führer. Woody Allen dealt with a similar premise a lot more playfully in his 1973 film *Sleeper,* in which a futuristic tyrant is killed by a bomb blast, leaving nothing behind but his nose – a nose that his followers hope to clone into a new leader. Even as the fiction of one decade becomes the technology of another, it is inevitable that this technology will be used – often by the wrong people.

If anything will prevent human cloning – whether of dictator, industrialist or baby daughter from becoming a reality, it's that science may not be able to clear the ethical high bar that would allow basic research to get under way in the first place. Cutting, coring and electrically jolting a sheep embryo is a huge moral distance from doing the same to a human embryo. It took 277 trials and errors to produce Dolly the sheep, creating a cellular body count that would look like sheer carnage if the cells were human. "Human beings ought never to be used as experimental subjects," Shapiro says simply.

Whether they will or not is impossible to say. Even if governments ban human cloning outright, it will not be so easy to police what goes on in private Laboratories that don't receive public money – or in pirate ones offshore. Years ago, Scottish scientists studying in vitro fertilization were subjected to such intense criticism that they took their work underground, continuing it in seclusion until they had the technology perfected.

zealous someone who is zealous does or supports something with great energy

to clear the bar in sports, i.e. highjump: to go over the bar without touching it

body count the number of dead soldiers after a period of fighting
carnage the violent killing of a large number of people
Shapiro the president of Princeton University, and chairman of President Clinton's ethics committee

in seclusion in isolation

Presumably, human-cloning researchers could also do their work on the sly, emerging only when they succeed.

Scientists do not pretend to know when that will happen, but some science observers fear it will be soon. The first infant clone could come squalling into the world within seven years, according to Arthur Caplan, director of the Center for Bioethics at the University of Pennsylvania. If he is right, science had better get its ethical house in order quickly. In calendar terms, seven years from now is a good way off, in scientific terms, it is tomorrow afternoon. *(563 words)*

from: *Time Magazine*, March 10, 1997

on the sly secretly

to squall to cry very loudly and noisily

Assignments

1. Describe how Dick Thompson sees the future of cloning technology.
2. Analyse the means the author uses to express his sceptical attitude towards the cloning of human beings.
3. Choose one of the following assignments:
   a) Write a personal comment on the following statement: "The first infant clone could be squalling into the world within seven years." (ll. 49f.)
   b) Imagine you are a woman or a man who is not able to have a baby in a natural way and you desperately want to have a child. How would you react to Shapiro's view that *"human beings ought never be used as experimental subjects"* (ll. 37f.)? You have the chance to discuss the issue with him. Write down the dialogue.

Erwartungshorizont zu Klausur 1

zu 1: After giving some examples of cloning from works of fiction, Dick Thompson expresses his fear that cloning technology might be used in the wrong way. He raises the question of whether the cloning of human beings is morally justifiable. To the author's mind, the government will be unable to prevent human cloning by law because scientists can always work secretly. Thus, it is the scientists who must be responsible for the future of this technology and who will have to find ethical agreements on human cloning. It is imperative to establish these agreements very soon because the possibility of cloning humans is not far off.

zu 2: The author voices his sceptical attitude towards the cloning of human beings by various means. First of all, the headline *"Will We Follow the Sheep?"* refers to the cloned sheep Dolly and suggests that it would be stupid to continue this research.
The structure of his argument also shows very clearly that he wants to sensitise the reader to the problems this technology could bring about. The author begins by conjuring up the fictional and frightening scene of an old despot who is happy to pass on his power because he knows that his country will be ruled according to his ideas by his clone after his death. He gives this idea support by referring to examples from history as well as from literature and film. He is convinced that this technology will be used and continues his train of thought by pointing out that human cloning is morally wrong. Once again, he gives an example (Dolly) and quotes an expert (Shapiro) to convince the reader of his opinion. When he states that the government is not able to control the development of science, he also makes use of an example (the Scottish scientists) to prove his point and concludes logically that the future use of cloning technology will depend on the scientists' ethics.
Furthermore, the author reveals his sceptical attitude by the choice of the following negative or disapproving words: *ultimate nightmare scenario* (l. 11), *body count* (l. 36), *sheer carnage* (l. 36) and *squalling* (l. 50).

zu 3a: Since this assignment requires a personal comment, answers will vary. It can be expected that students will present arguments from the fields of ethics, medicine or religion to support their opinions.

zu 3b: The assignment offers the chance to voice positive as well as negative attitudes towards the cloning of human beings. Students can discuss ethical, medical and religious ideas. Since the text is a dialogue, spoken language forms should be accepted.

The squalor of that little house on the outskirts of the pueblo!
A space of dust and rubbish separated it from the village. Two famine-stricken dogs were nosing obscenely in the garbage at its door. Inside, when they entered, the twilight stank and was loud with flies.
"Linda!" the young man called.
From the inner room a rather hoarse female voice said, "Coming."
They waited. In bowls on the floor were the remains of a meal, perhaps of several meals.
The door opened. A very stout blonde squaw stepped across the threshold and stood looking at the strangers, staring incredulously, her mouth open. Lenina noticed with disgust that two of the front teeth were missing. And the colour of the ones that remained … She shuddered. It was worse than the old man. So fat, and all the lines in her face, the flabbiness, the wrinkles. And the sagging cheeks, with those purplish blotches. And the red veins on her nose, the bloodshot eyes. And that neck – that neck; and the blanket she wore over her head – ragged and filthy. And under the brown sack-shaped tunic those enormous breasts, the bulge of the stomach, the hips. Oh, much worse than the old man, much worse! And suddenly the creature burst out in a torrent of speech, rushed at her with outstretched arms and – Ford! Ford! It was too revolting, in another moment she'd be sick – pressed her against the bulge, the bosom, and began to kiss her. Ford! To *kiss*, slobberingly and smelt too horrible, obviously never had a bath, and simply reeked of that beastly stuff that was put in Delta and Epsilon bottles (no, it wasn't true about Bernard), positively stank of alcohol. She broke away as quickly as she could.
A blubbered and distorted face confronted her; the creature was crying.
"Oh, my dear, my dear." The torrent of words flowed sobbingly. "If you knew how glad – after all these years! A civilized face. Yes, and civilized clothes. Because I thought I should never see a piece of real acetate silk again." She fingered the sleeve of Lenina's shirt. The nails were black. "And those adorable viscose velveteen shorts! Do you know, dear, I've still got my old clothes, the ones I came in, put away in a box. I'll show them you afterwards. Though, of course, the acetate has all gone into holes. But such a lovely white bandolier – though I must say your green morocco is even lovelier. Not that it did me much good, that bandolier." Her tears began to flow again. "I suppose John told you. What I had to suffer – and not a gramme of *soma* to be had. Only a drink of *mescal* every now and then, when Popé used to bring it. Popé is a boy I used to know. But it makes you feel so bad afterwards, the *mescal* does, and you're sick with the *peyotl*; besides it always made that awful feeling of being ashamed much worse the next day. And I was so ashamed. Just think of it: me, a Beta – having a baby: put yourself in my place." (The mere suggestion made Lenina shudder.) *(527 words)*

from: Aldous Huxley, *Brave New World*, pp. 150–152;

squalor *Schmutz*
hoarse *heiser*
flabbiness *Schwammigkeit*
sagging *Hänge-*
blotch *Fleck*
ragged *zerlumpt*
bulge *Wölbung*
slobberingly *sabbernd, feucht*
blubbered *verheult* (to blubber – *flennen*)
velveteen *samtartig*
mescal *tequilaähnlicher Schnaps aus dem Saft von Agaven, deren Spitzen aufgrund ihres Gehalts an dem Halluzinogen Meskalin als Rauschmittel gekaut werden*
peyotl *aztekische Bezeichnung für die Mescalpflanze*

Assignments

1. Describe in your own words what Lenina finds in the little house on the outskirts of the pueblo.
2. Explain the following expressions from the text:
   - l. 19: "Ford! Ford!"
   - ll. 22f.: "Delta and Epsilon bottles"
   - l. 23: "no, it wasn't true about Bernard"
   - l. 35: "gramme of *soma*"
   - ll. 39f.: "I was so ashamed … me, a Beta – having a baby."
3. Which stylistic devices does the author use to show how revolting Linda and her surroundings are to Lenina?
4. Creative task: You are Lenina. Report to your friends back home what you have encountered.
   or
   Comment: Consider the society we live in today. Would life as described in *Brave New World* be desirable?

Erwartungshorizont zu Klausur 2

zu 1: the house stinks and is very dirty/soiled
there are leftovers on the floor
there is probably no bathroom because Linda definitely smells bad and has dirty fingernails

zu 2: "Ford! Ford!": people in *Brave New World* believe in Ford, not in God
"Delta and Epsilon bottles": people are not born, but bred in bottles according to the future jobs they are supposed to hold. Delta and Epsilon people do very low work and are not very intelligent due to doses of alcohol that are injected into their breeding bottles.
"no, it wasn't true about Bernard": people are gossiping about Bernard having had some alcohol put into his bottle because he is different from them
"gramme of *soma*": people are taking a chemical drug called *soma* that makes them very relaxed and happy
"I was so ashamed...": Linda refers to the fact that women in the *Brave New World* no longer conceive and give birth, and instead regard that process as disgusting and very old-fashioned

zu 3: l. 4: twilight stank...was loud with flies → personification/metaphor
ll. 7/8: remains of meals...several meals → climax
ll. 11–18: And...(repeated 7 times) → polysyndeton
l. 13: lines...face...wrinkles → enumeration/asyndeton
l. 15: that neck – that neck → repetition
l. 17: breasts...stomach...hips → enumeration/asyndeton
ll. 17/18: Oh, much worse...much worse → exclamation/repetition
ll. 20/21: the bulge, the bosom, and began to → alliteration
ll. 22/23: simply reeked...positively stank → climax
l. 25: creature → derogatory expression
The fact that this passage is written from Lenina's point of view helps to underline her personal horror at what she is seeing. Lenina is deeply shocked by the reality she experiences on the reservation – she is afraid of being sick. The paradoxon "real acetate silk" used by Linda is a typical pun used by Huxley in order to make fun of the civilized world of *Brave New World*.

zu 4: creative task: answers will vary – however, Lenina's disgust and total rejection of what she has seen must be expressed clearly.
comment: answers will vary – however, critical aspects such as totalitarian government, no free will, rigid caste system and drug abuse as means of manipulating people should be mentioned and contrasted with our democratic system.

Konzeption des Unterrichtsmodells

Der Roman *Brave New World* hat seit Jahrzehnten seinen festen Platz im Curriculum der Oberstufe an deutschen Schulen. Er bietet Jugendlichen die Gelegenheit, sich mit dem Problem der unendlichen Möglichkeiten, die sich aus der rasanten Entwicklung der Gentechnologien ergeben, auseinander zu setzen. Obwohl 1932 erschienen, wirkt der Roman keineswegs verstaubt oder überholt, sondern – erschreckenderweise – brandaktuell. Es scheint durchaus denkbar, die Bearbeitung des Romans fächerübergreifend mit Biologie und Philosophie/Religion abzusprechen, da auch in diesen Fächern über Probleme der Gentechnologie gesprochen werden kann. Im Englischunterricht kann und soll nicht auf die biologisch-technischen Einzelheiten des Klonvorgangs eingegangen werden, dies ist auch keinesfalls nötig, um sich eine Meinung zu der Thematik bilden zu können. Dagegen scheint es sinnvoll, die Schwerpunkte auf weitere Themen wie Drogen in unserer Gesellschaft, Beeinflussung der Menschen durch Medien, die Arbeitsweise der Medien, unser Freizeit- und Konsumverhalten zu legen.

Die *Einstiegsseite* (S. 3) wird am besten auf Folie kopiert und dem Kurs vor der Lektüre per Overhead-Projektor präsentiert. Es soll spekuliert werden, worum es in dem zu lesenden Roman *Brave New World* geht.

Das vorliegende Unterrichtsmodell thematisiert ausgewählte Aspekte des Romans, die in den einzelnen *Components* bearbeitet werden. Die 288 Seiten der Reclamausgabe sollen vom Kurs vor der eigentlichen Bearbeitung der *Components 2–5* gelesen werden. Diese Vorarbeit sollte nicht mehr als drei Wochen in Anspruch nehmen. Als Begleitung der Lektüre dienen die *Worksheets* aus ***Component 1***, die mit den unterschiedlichsten Aufgabentypen wie Fragen beantworten, Tabellen ergänzen, falsch oder richtig angeben, Lückentexte ausfüllen, Reihenfolge von Sätzen festlegen u.a. überprüfen, ob die Leser den Text verstanden haben. Die neun *Worksheets* können entweder sukzessive begleitend zur Lektüre besprochen werden, oder jeweils zwei bis drei *Worksheets* werden vor der Bearbeitung der einzelnen *Components 2–5* besprochen. Die Einstiegsseite kann ebenfalls mit der Besprechung eines *Worksheets* verknüpft werden, hier böte sich vor allem *Worksheet 1* an. Es ist keineswegs zwingend, dass alle Schülerinnen und Schüler alle *Worksheets* bearbeiten, obwohl sie in der Regel die Bearbeitung der *Worksheets* als motivierend und hilfreich bei der Lektüre empfinden.
Denkbar wäre, dass einzelne Schülerinnen und Schüler oder Schülergruppen einzelne Kapitel mithilfe der *Worksheets* vorstellen. Die Ergebnisse der Arbeit an den *Worksheets* könnten im Kurs ausgehängt werden, um allen Kursmitgliedern die Chance zu geben, sich lektürebegleitend zu orientieren. Ferner kann man die Aufgabe stellen, dass einzelne Kursteilnehmer eine bestimmte Anzahl von Vokabeln aus ihnen zugewiesenen Kapiteln zusammenstellen und als Lernvokabular der Lerngruppe zur Verfügung stellen.

Component 2 behandelt zwei Themenschwerpunkte, zum einen eine kurze Einführung in das Genre Dystopia, das heute häufig in Filmen bearbeitet wird. Daher bietet sich ein kurzer Exkurs in die Filmpräsentation an, der erfahrungsgemäß die Schülerinnen und Schüler sehr motiviert. Als Hilfestellung dazu bietet das Modell ein *Worksheet* zum Thema Filmpräsentation. Zum anderen bietet es ein Expertenpuzzle mit fünf unterschiedlich schwierigen und langen Texten, die der Kurs in arbeitsteiliger Gruppenarbeit bearbeiten soll. Diese Texte bieten unterschiedliche Meinungen zum Thema Gentechnik. Das Verständnis der Texte wird abschließend mit einem kleinen Test überprüft.

Im sich anschließenden ***Component 3*** geht es vor allem um das Thema Konditionierung. Dabei werden kurze Einblicke in die bedeutendsten Vertreter der klassischen Konditionierung (Pavlov) und des Behaviorismus (Watson) gegeben und die Wirkung ihrer Forschungen am Beispiel der Werbung dargestellt. Dazu werden Texte aus einer Online-Enzyklopädie und einer Multimedia-Enzyklopädie herangezogen, anhand derer die Schülerinnen und Schüler ihre Fertigkeiten der gezielten Informationsentnahme schulen und die Erkenntnisse auf die Praktiken übertragen können, die in *Brave New World* beschrieben werden. Eine Interpretation der Konditionierungsszene erfolgt in kreativer Form, indem ein *Storyboard* für einen möglichen Film gezeichnet wird. Zur Verdeutlichung der Techniken, die im Verfahren der „Hypnopädie“ angewendet werden, wird den Schülerinnen und Schülern die Gelegenheit gegeben, diese in einem kleinen Experiment selbst zu erfahren. Den Abschluss von *Component 3* bildet ein „halbes Kreuzworträtsel“, anhand dessen das themenspezifische Vokabular des Romans in spielerischer Form umgewälzt wird.

Component 4 konzentriert sich auf Themen wie Einsatz von Drogen, Gestaltung der Freizeit und Rolle der Medien als Mittel des Weltstaates, seine Bürger zu manipulieren und somit unter Kontrolle zu halten. Eine Gruppenarbeitsphase soll die Schülerinnen und Schüler zu selbstständigem Lernen anregen und ihre sozialen Kompetenzen stärken sowie das Präsentieren von Arbeitsergebnissen und deren Evaluation trainieren. Die sich anschließende Untersuchung der Arbeitsweise der Medien hat einen analytischen Schwerpunkt. Zunächst werden die stilistischen Mittel des Romans aufgedeckt, mit denen der Autor die Praktiken der Massenmedien kritisiert. Danach wird durch die Analyse von zwei Filmszenen geklärt, welche filmischen Mittel dieselbe Funktion erfüllen. Ein Vergleich mit den Gegebenheiten in unserer heutigen Gesellschaft rundet das Thema ab.

Component 5 ist so angelegt, dass er auch als Lernzirkel eingesetzt werden kann. Er bietet unterschiedliche Materialien, die die vier Grundfertigkeiten Lesen, Schreiben, Hören und Sprechen schulen sollen. Durch verschiedene Sozialformen sollen die Teamfähigkeit und die Lernerautonomie der Schülerinnen und Schüler gefördert werden. Eine Tabelle am Beginn des *Components* ermöglicht der Lehrkraft eine schnelle Orientierung für die Auswahl, falls man nicht den kompletten Zirkel nutzen, sondern nur einzelne Aufgaben bearbeiten lassen möchte.

Component 1: Understanding the Novel

Bevor mit der Arbeit an dem Roman *Brave New World* begonnen wird, sollen die Schülerinnen und Schüler eigenständig das Buch gelesen haben. Die Bearbeitung von *while-reading tasks* kann sehr hilfreich sein, wenn man sicherstellen möchte, dass die zur häuslichen Lektüre aufgegebenen Kapitel auch wirklich gelesen wurden. Daher finden sich im Folgenden *Worksheets*, auf welchen Aufgaben zu jedem einzelnen Kapitel des Romans gestellt sind. Die Menge an Text, die als Hausaufgabe gelesen werden sollte, ist abhängig vom Leistungsstand der Gruppe.
Die 288 Seiten der Reclamausgabe (mit Hilfen) sollten von den Mitgliedern eines Leistungskurses in zwei Wochen, von einem Grundkurs in gut drei Wochen bewältigt werden können. Während der Bearbeitung der folgenden *Components* werden dann einzelne Kapitel erneut zu Hause von den Schülerinnen und Schülern gelesen werden müssen, damit sie in der Lage sind, über bestimmte Textpassagen detailliert im Unterricht sprechen zu können.
Alternativ kann die Lektüre auch parallel zur Bearbeitung der Aufgaben in den weiteren *Components* erfolgen, allerdings muss man dann bei der Menge der zu stellenden Hausaufgaben Abstriche machen.
Die Einstiegsseite wird auf Folie kopiert und dem Kurs vor dem Beginn der Lektüre vorgelegt. Eine *Brainstorming*-Phase soll die Schülerinnen und Schüler auf das Thema des Romans einstimmen.

Look at this picture and speculate on what the topic of the novel *Brave New World* might be.

- artists and their models
- people being all the same
- making everybody look alike – cosmetic surgery
- genetic engineering
- …

Die Einstiegsseite kann auch gezeigt werden, nachdem der Kurs den Roman gelesen hat. Die Aufgabe besteht dann darin, einen Bezug zwischen Roman und Bild herzustellen.

Look at this picture and explain in which way it relates to *Brave New World*.

- As in the novel, all these people look alike.
- From one person, many more identical people are derived.
- Whereas the top men have got eyes, the clones are eyeless.
- …

Chapter I

1. Find five words in chapter I that you think are remarkable.

2. Explain the meaning of the following expressions:
   - Bokanovsky's Process (p. 24)
   - freemartins (p. 33)
   - conditioning (p. 37)

Chapter II

Answer the following questions:

Delta babies are prevented from enjoying flowers or books (p. 44).

1. Why?
2. How?

The lower classes are conditioned to love all country sports (p. 45).

3. Why?

The students blush when the word "parent" is used by the Director (p. 45).

4. Why?

Reuben Rabinovitch helped to develop the technique of sleep-teaching or hypnopaedia (p. 46).

5. How?

Moral education can be achieved by hypnopaedia (p. 49).

6. Why?

Find information about:

1. George Bernard Shaw
2. Henry Ford
3. Model T

Worksheet 2

Chapter III

Fill in information in this table:

	Past (= our Present)	Present (= our Future)
erotic play of children (p. 52)		
adolescents' erotic games (p. 55)		
Government (p. 57)		
attitude towards history (p. 57)		
family life (p. 60)		
pat on the behind (p. 66)		
emotions (p. 68)		
beliefs (p. 71)		
proverbs (p. 74)		

Chapter III (cont.)

From p. 76 to p. 81 there is a mixture of dialogues. Identify the speakers of the following utterances:

1. “Well, all I can say is that I'm going to accept his invitation.” (p. 72)
2. “The Nine Years' War, the Great Economic Collapse. There was a choice between World Control and destruction.” (p. 73)
3. “Not nearly so pneumatic as Lenina. Oh, not nearly.” (p. 74)
4. “I do love flying. I do love flying.” (p. 75)
5. “There were some things called the pyramids, for example.” (p. 76)
6. “I've had it nearly three months.” (p. 77)
7. “And what makes it worse, she thinks of herself as meat.” (p. 78)
8. “Stability was practically assured.” (p. 79)

Collect information about:

1. Leo Trotsky
2. Mustapha Kemal Pascha
3. H. G. Wells
4. Sigmund Freud

Chapter IV

Right or wrong?

1. Lenina only loves Henry Foster.
2. Bernard is embarrassed when Lenina publicly accepts his invitation to go to New Mexico with him.
3. An Epsilon-Minus Semi-Moron is an especially well-educated person.
4. Benito Hoover is a very glum man.
5. The Red Rocket Service is an Atlantic service flying from New York to London.
6. Lenina likes the colour khaki.

You meet Mr Helmholtz Watson.

1. What is his job?
2. Is he talented?
3. What is his problem?
4. What is his relationship to Bernard Marx?

Chapter V

1. What does a fun day look like for Lenina and Henry?

2. Fill in the missing words:

Bernard rushes to the ________________________. In that building there are ________________ rooms for Solidarity Groups that hold their ________________ services there. He meets ________________________ there, who is disappointed because he did not do any ______________________ or ______________________ that afternoon. The purpose of the meeting at the Singery is for each member of the group to lose his or her ________________________. The procedure of taking ________________________ in the form of tablets and in a cup of ______________________ resembles the Christian ________________________. You can see that the hymns and the *soma* have started to work because the participants' ____________________ shine, their __________________ are flushed and they all have __________________ faces. For Bernard, however, the _________________ is far away. He knows that neither the hymns nor the *soma* will make him __________________ a member of the group. All members of his group can hear the ____________________ of the ____________________ and they all start to ________________________. Everybody is ________________________, only Bernard feels even more ________________________.

Chapter VI

Complete the following sentences:

1. Lenina hates the North Pole because …
2. Bernard does not want to go for a swim at the Torquay Country Club because …
3. Bernard does not want to have any *soma* because …
4. Lenina does not enjoy the quietness of the evening because …
5. Bernard makes love to Lenina because …
6. The director remembers his long-ago visit to the Reservation when …
7. The Director does not want Bernard to think that …
8. The Director warns Bernard because …
9. Lenina is very eager to go to the Reservation although …
10. The warden tells them that …
11. Bernard is terribly upset when he learns from Helmholtz that …
12. The savages will not do any harm because …

Chapter VII

Put the sentences in the correct order:

1. Lenina is shocked by the apparition of two painted Indians who are carrying snakes.
2. The English-speaking savage seems to fall for Lenina.
3. Lenina enjoys the Indian drums because they remind her of the solidarity services.
4. Linda is very happy to meet other civilized people though Lenina feels revolted by her.
5. Lenina does not like the Indian guide who accompanies them to the pueblo of Malpais.
6. Linda remembers all the hypnopaedic sentences and feels bad about her current condition.
7. The harmless dance becomes dangerous when a lot of black snakes are handed out.
8. The climb up to the pueblo is very steep and hard on the walkers.
9. From what the English-speaking savage tells them, Lenina and Bernard deduce that he must be the Director's son, born in Malpais.
10. Lenina cannot understand how the natives can live in such dirt.
11. Linda explains that she was very upset to have ended up stuck at the reservation and having to have a baby.
12. Lenina and Bernard witness a strange ritual: A boy is whipped senseless and suddenly all Indians flee the square.
13. Linda tells Lenina about the difficulties of raising a child in the wilderness.
14. Finally, they arrive at the village square.
15. Linda tells Lenina that she had fights with the Indian women because she adhered to the principle: "Everybody belongs to every one else."
16. Lenina and Bernard marvel at the sight of a very old and frail Indian as they never see such old people in their civilized world.
17. After the ritual hitting of the young man, they meet a savage who speaks English.
18. Bernard, in contrast to Lenina, enjoys the sight of breast-feeding mothers.

Chapter VIII

Combine the sentences:

1. Bernard asks	a. when Linda was sent away by the Indian women because she could not weave.
2. John tells him about an incident	b. to read, but she does not have anything interesting to read.
3. John remembers another event	c. of the Other Place and the wonderful things you can do there.
4. Once Popé visited Linda	d. he suddenly feels reminded of Hamlet and tries to stab Popé.
5. One day, three women came to Linda	e. when the girl he loves is married to another man.
6. John remembers Linda's tales	f. a very old book for John to read – Shakespeare's *Complete Works.*
7. He also tells Bernard about the stories	g. John is excluded; the Indians throw stones at him.
8. Linda teaches John	h. John to explain his life-style to him.
9. John wants to know	i. one of the Indians teaches him to work the clay.
10. One day, Popé brings	j. and punished her with a whip.
11. When John sees Popé in bed with his mother,	k. and brought a bottle of alcohol, which made Linda quite drunk.
12. When John is fifteen,	l. take John and Linda with him to London.
13. John is unhappy	m. that they are both feeling alone in their societies.
14. When the initiation rite is performed,	n. much more than Linda can explain.
15. John and Bernard find out	o. when Linda had a visitor and he was brought to another room.
16. Bernard decides to	p. he heard from one of the old men in the pueblo and how his and his mother's stories mixed.

Chapter IX

1. What does Lenina dream about on her *soma* holiday?
2. Write down John's inner monologue when he finds Lenina and Bernard's door locked and thinks that they have left for London without him.

Chapter X

Add the speaker's thoughts when he/she utters the following sentences:

1. "Good morning, Director. You asked me to come and speak to you here." (p. 183)
2. "Marx, can you show any reason why I should not now execute the judgement passed upon you?" (p. 185)
3. "Certainly. But it's in the passage. One moment. Come in." (p. 185)
4. "Did you think I didn't recognize him?" (p. 185)
5. "My father!" (p. 187)

Chapter XI

Describe the differences between the two savages:

Linda	John

1. In which ways does Bernard Marx change in people's estimation now that he is the Savage's guardian?
2. What has changed in Lenina's life due to her acquaintance with Bernard Marx and John?

Chapter XII

Which expressions referring to Bernard show how deeply humiliated he is at his own party when John does not attend?

Bernard is reunited in his friendship with the Savage and Helmholtz.

1. Why has Helmholtz had some difficulties with the authorities?
2. Explain why Helmholtz finds the scene from *Romeo and Juliet* so exhilarating (p. 224).
3. What does Helmholtz call Shakespeare?
4. What does he compare him to?
5. Can you explain that term?

Chapter XIII

1. Fill in the other half of the dialogue on the phone (p. 239).
2. Lenina is too ashamed to tell her friend Fanny about what has happened, however, she writes down in her diary how terribly wrong her meeting with John went.

Chapter XIV

1. Describe the atmosphere in which Linda is dying.
2. How do the "civilized" people react towards John's display of grief?

Chapter XV

You are one of the Deltas waiting for the distribution of *soma* when you suddenly see John, the Savage. Write an interior monologue describing the following scene.

Chapter XVI

Right or wrong?

1. Mustapha Mond is obviously stupid and cruel.
2. Shakespeare is prohibited because his plays are beautiful.
3. There cannot be any new plays like *Othello* because everybody is happy.
4. There are plans to form a purely Alpha society.
5. Workers are happy with their 7 $^1/_2$ hours of unexhausting labour.
6. Art is sacrificed to make sure that there will be stability in society, but science must be developed further.
7. Bernard Marx behaves like a madman when he learns that he is to be sent to Iceland.
8. Mustapha Mond is surprised that, in the past, people believed that scientific progress could go on indefinitely.
9. Mustapha Mond tells Helmholtz that he has to go to Samosa.

Chapter XVII

Tick the correct statements:

1. The Controller has got a collection of
   A. poetry of the 19th century.
   B. novels of the 20th century.
   C. religious books.

2. Religious sentiment is superfluous because
   A. there is eternal youth and prosperity.
   B. Ford has become the new God.
   C. new philosophers have proven that there is no God.

3. The fact that nobody has to be noble or chaste in the modern world
   A. amuses John.
   B. horrifies John.
   C. horrifies the Controller.

4. *Soma* is
   A. a very dangerous drug.
   B. very helpful for finding the enemies of civilization.
   C. Christianity without tears.

5. In civilized countries there are no mosquitoes because
   A. after the last war they all died.
   B. genetic engineering has got rid of them.
   C. there are effective pesticides.

6. The V.P.S. treatment is compulsory
   A. because human beings need adrenin in order to remain healthy.
   B. because it is part of the conditioning process.
   C. although it can be quite harmful to people's adrenals.

Chapter XVIII

1. Bernard Marx and Helmholtz Watson are expelled from civilization. Write a short article about them for the *Brave New World* Chronicle, informing their Alpha colleagues about their fate.

2. Write an obituary about John for the same newspaper.

Lösungen zu Worksheet 1:

Chapter I:

1. possible words: A.F. 632; Director of Hatchery and Conditioning; Alphas, Betas…; Podsnap's Technology; Fertilizing / Bottling Room; Embryo Store; Decanting Room
2.
   - Bokanovsky's Process: By this process one egg will divide into eight to ninety-six identical eggs and thus develop into up to ninety-six adults.
   - freemartins: People who look like women but who are sterile.
   - conditioning: By manipulating the embryos, the behaviour of the adults can be influenced.

Chapter II:

1. Books are not good for Deltas because lower-caste people could read something that is not good for them, that could give them wrong ideas. Deltas used to enjoy nature, however, they only spent money on transport. In other words, nature has one big disadvantage: it is free.
2. When they are eight months old they are repeatedly shown pictures of flowers. If they try to reach out to the flowers, bells, sirens and loud explosions are sounded so that the babies become very scared. In addition, they receive mild electric shocks, which kill all their joy of nature.
3. Because of economic policy. For these sports you need all kinds, of complicated equipment, which must be bought.
4. The students are embarrassed because for them the words "parent" or "viviparous" describe a form of recreation that is abnormal to them. They feel slightly disgusted by the idea of women giving birth.
5. He was left alone by his parents after he listened to an English lecture by George Bernard Shaw, which he could repeat the next morning word for word.
6. Irrational ways of thinking can be implanted because they do not need a basis in science. If you are told that brown is an ugly colour thousands of times, sooner or later you will believe it. Words without a rational basis can be implanted more easily than scientific knowledge.

Information:

1. George Bernard Shaw (1856–1950)
   Shaw was an Irish dramatist, literary critic and a socialist spokesman. His father was an alcoholic, which prompted Shaw to become a teetotaller. At the age of 15, he started to work as a clerk. In 1876, he left Ireland for London and did not return for another thirty years. In 1884, he joined the socialist Fabian Society. His most famous works include *Pygmalion* and *Saint Joan*. In his plays, he combines contemporary moral problems with an ironic tone and numerous paradoxes ("Shavian wit").

2. Henry Ford (1863–1947)
   Ford was born as the son of a farmer in Michigan. He left school at the age of 15 and worked as an apprentice in a machine shop in Detroit. Motivated by an article about Nicholas Otto, a German who had built an internal combustion engine, Ford worked on the development of a petrol-driven motor car. After several failed attempts to start his own business, he finally succeeded in establishing his car factory in 1907. In 1909, he decided to produce only one car – the Model T. Ford was strongly opposed to World War I and tried to get politicians in Europe and the US to negotiate peace treaties. By 1925, Ford

was producing 60% of America's total output of cars. Although he also opposed America's going to war in World War II, he supported his country by producing bombers during the war.

3. Model T
   The first production Model T Ford was assembled in Detroit on October 1st, 1908. With the Model T, Ford succeeded in building a car for the masses, producing 15,000,000 automobiles from 1908 – 1927. By using moving assembly lines for his car production, Ford was able to assemble a car in one hour, 33 minutes. Often, the Model T has been called the car of the century due to its impact on society and industry.

Lösungen zu Worksheet 2:

Chapter III:

	Past (= our Present)	Present (= our Future)
erotic play of children (p. 52)	immoral, abnormal	children play naked, sexual games are encouraged
adolescents' erotic games (p. 55)	abnormal	normal past time
Government (p. 57)	Presidents/Kings of nations	Controller for Western Europe/Ford
Attitude towards history (p. 57)	history was very important	history is bunk, it is not taught
family life (p. 60)	home, a few small rooms, no air, no space, darkness, disease, smells, monogamy	promiscuity, no relationships, pregnancy substitutes, "every one belongs to every one else"
pat on the behind (p. 66)	insult	conventionality
emotions (p. 68)	horrible because people were thrown into turmoil by emotions all the time	preserve people from having emotions – try to fulfil a desire as soon as it arises
beliefs (p. 71)	there was Christianity, and women were forced to give birth; Governments prohibited new technologies, democracy	clean recreation, no strings attached, consumption
proverbs (p. 74)	mending was better than spending the less stitches, the more riches	ending is better than spending the more stitches, the less riches

Lösungen zu Worksheet 3:

Chapter III (cont.):

From p. 76 to p. 81 there is a mixture of dialogues. Identify the speakers of the following utterances:

1. "Well, all I can say is that I'm going to accept his invitation." (p. 72)
   Lenina
2. "The Nine Years' War, the Great Economic Collapse. There was a choice between World Control and destruction." (p. 73)
   Mustapha Mond
3. "Not nearly so pneumatic as Lenina. Oh, not nearly." (p. 74)
   Henry Foster
4. "I do love flying. I do love flying." (p. 75)
   voices for babies
5. "There were some things called the pyramids, for example." (p. 76)
   Mustapha Mond
6. "I've had it nearly three months." (p. 77)
   Fanny
7. "And what makes it worse, she thinks of herself as meat." (p. 78)
   Bernard Marx
8. "Stability was practically assured." (p. 79)
   Mustapha Mond

Information:

1. Leo Trotsky (1879–1940)
   Trotsky was a Russian revolutionary who joined the Bolshevik party and took part in seizing power in 1917. Stalin defeated him in 1924 during the struggles for power following Lenin's death. Further problems with the Communist Party led to his exile in 1929. He moved to Mexico, where he was assassinated at Stalin's command.
2. Mustapha Kemal Pascha (1881–1938)
   Kemal was a Turkish politician and general and the first president of Turkey from 1923 onwards.
   For joining a revolutionary society, Kemal was banished in 1904. However, he was later pardoned and even promoted in the army and was very successful in defending the Dardanelles against the British in 1915. In 1921, he led the Turkish armies against the Greeks, defeating them and expelling them from Turkey. In the aftermath of these events, the Turkish republic was proclaimed and he became its first president. In 1934, he assumed the name Atatürk, meaning "Father of the Turks".
3. H(erbert) G(eorge) Wells (1866–1946)
   Wells was a novelist, journalist, sociologist, and historian whose science-fiction stories have been filmed many times, e.g. *The Time Machine* (1895) and *The War of the Worlds* (1898). Before becoming a full-time writer (1893), Wells was a teacher at a private school. Wells' novels are highly entertaining; nevertheless, he also tries to make his audience think about the future of mankind. In 1903, he joined the socialist Fabian Society in London, which was led by George Bernard Shaw. Although he quarrelled with his fellow members, he remained loyal to their common cause.
4. Sigmund Freud (1856–1939)
   Freud was the founding father of psychoanalysis, one of the most influential schools of psychology. His mother, who was the second wife of his father, a

Jewish wool merchant, was also 20 years younger than her husband. Freud had two older half-brothers and seven younger siblings. Freud entered the University of Vienna at the age of 17 in order to study medicine. He spent most of his life in that city until he had to flee to England in 1938 because of the Nazi invasion. He published *Studies in Hysteria* (1895), *The Interpretation of Dreams* (1900) and *Three Essays on the Theory of Sexuality* (1905) and became one of the most famous psychologists of our times.

Chapter IV:

Right or wrong?
1. wrong
2. right
3. wrong
4. wrong
5. right
6. wrong

Questions about Mr Helmholtz Watson:
1. He is lecturer at the College of Emotional Engineering; he composes feely scenarios and invents hypnopaedic logos and slogans.
2. He is actually too talented for his job, whatever that means.
3. He has found out that sport, women and communal activities are only second best without knowing what is best.
4. They are friends. He tells Bernard about his doubts; however, when Bernard shows emotions, he is quite embarrassed.

Lösungen zu Worksheet 4:

Chapter V:

1. What does a fun day look like for Lenina and Henry?

- Obstacle golf
- take some *soma*
- spend the night at a club where they can enjoy London's finest Scent and Colour Organ and dance to the latest synthetic music
- have sex

2. Fill in the missing words:

Bernard rushes to the *Ford Community Singery*. In that building there are *7000* rooms for Solidarity Groups that hold their *fortnightly* services there. He meets *Morgana Rothschild* there, who is disappointed because he did not do any *Obstacle golf* or *Electro-magnetic golf* that afternoon. The purpose of the meeting at the Singery is for each member of the group to lose his or her *identity*. The procedure of taking *soma* in the form of tablets and in a cup of *strawberry ice-cream* resembles the Christian *last supper*. You can see that the hymns and the *soma* have started to work because the participants' *eyes* shine, their *cheeks* are flushed and they all have *happy* faces. For Bernard, however, the *Coming* is far away. He knows that neither the hymns nor the *soma* will make him *become* a member of the group. All members of his group can hear the *Feet* of the *Greater Being* and they all start to *dance*. Everybody is *satisfied*, only Bernard feels even more *isolated*.

Chapter VI:

Complete the following sentences:

1. Lenina hates the North Pole because *there is nothing to do and the hotel is too old-fashioned.*
2. Bernard does not want to go for a swim at the Torquay Country Club because *he does not like crowds.*
3. Bernard does not want to have any *soma* because *he would rather be himself in a bad mood than somebody else.*
4. Lenina does not enjoy the quietness of the evening because *she cannot help preferring to be a member of a crowd due to her being conditioned that way.*
5. Bernard makes love to Lenina because *he knows she expects that of him.*
6. The director remembers his long-ago visit to the Reservation when *his girlfriend unexpectedly got lost.*
7. The Director does not want Bernard to think that *he had any indecorous relationship with the girl, meaning there was nothing emotional.*
8. The Director warns Bernard because *he has had reports of Bernard's non-infantile behaviour.*
9. Lenina is very eager to go to the Reservation although *Bernard warns her that there will be no amenities such as Escalator Squash TV.*
10. The warden tells them that *people are still born in the Reservation.*
11. Bernard is terribly upset when he learns from Helmholtz that *the Director seems to have decided to send him to Iceland.*
12. The savages will not do any harm because *they know they will be attacked if they try to hurt civilized people.*

Lösungen zu Worksheet 5:

Chapter VII:

the correct order: 5 – 8 – 1 – 10 – 16 – 18 – 14 – 3 – 7 – 12 – 17 – 2 – 9 – 4 – 11 – 6 – 15 – 13

Lösungen zu Worksheet 6:

Chapter VIII:

Lösung: 1 – h; 2 – o; 3 – a; 4 – k; 5 – j; 6 – c; 7 – p; 8 – b; 9 – n; 10 – f; 11 – d; 12 – i; 13 – e; 14 – g; 15 – m; 16 – l

Chapter IX:

1. Answers will vary.
2. John's thoughts should centre on his anxiety about being left alone in a world he does not understand. In addition to that, he should reflect on his feelings for Lenina.

Lösungen zu Worksheet 7:

Chapter X:

Answers will vary.

Chapter XI:

Describe the differences between the two savages:

Linda	John
– not a "real" savage	– handsome, young
– bad teeth, bad complexion	– shows little astonishment at civilized inventions
– screaming, only tolerable when on *soma*-holiday	– does not take any *soma*
not interesting to people	interesting character

1. In which ways does Bernard Marx change in people's estimation now that he is the Savage's guardian?
   - is begged for invitations by important people
   - can have all the women he wants to have
   - loses his friend Helmholtz
   - does not find the world unsatisfactory any longer
   - criticizes the social order openly, emphasizes his unorthodoxy
   - even dares to lecture Mustapha Mond about the social order

2. What has changed in Lenina's life due to her acquaintance with Bernard Marx and John?
   - she has been asked by the Secretary of the Young Women's Fordian Association to give a speech about her experiences
   - she has appeared on TV
   - she is being dated by the most desirable men
   - she has been to France with the Deputy Governor of the Bank of Europe
   - she has not made love to the Savage, which distresses her greatly

Chapter XII:

Which expressions referring to Bernard show how deeply humiliated he is at his own party when John does not attend?

p. 211: shrink back, diminished
insignificant fellow with the unsavoury reputation
wretched little man
creature with a Gamma-Minus physique

p. 213: transferring him to Iceland
the tight balloon of Bernard's happy self-confidence was leaking from a thousand wounds
pale, distraught, abject and agitated
stammering, incoherent apologies
begging them to sit down

p. 214: they duly ate, but ignored him
rude to his face
moment of his greatest humiliation

p. 215: he stammering repeated
punctured, utterly defeated, … begins to weep
uses 4 tablets of *soma*

Bernard is reunited in his friendship with the Savage and Helmholtz.
1. He wrote a poem praising solitude, which is, of course, against the rules.
2. The whole idea of natural parents is funny to a person who has been raised in the new circumstances of Huxley's *"Brave New World"*. This is basically an example of a cultural clash.
3. "that old fellow"
4. "marvellous propaganda technician"
5. Answers will vary.

Lösungen zu Worksheet 8:

Chapter XIII:

1. Fill in the other half of the dialogue on the phone (p. 239):
   - Hello, is this John?
   - Are you John, the Savage?
   - So you are the Savage.
   - I don't know if you're interested, but there is someone very ill here.
   - I think it is your mother. She is not well.
   - To a hospital.
   - Three Park Lane.
2. Lenina's diary entry: Answers will vary.

Chapter XIV:

1. - TV
   - changing perfume
   - first-class hotel
   - feely palace
   - Super-Vox-Wurlitzerania talks
   - no personal visitor
   - *soma*-induced happiness
   - second infancy
   - group of children come in order to be death-conditioned
2. - the scandalous exhibition (p. 249)
   - shocking scene
   - The nurse is primarily concerned about what John's behaviour might mean for the children.
   - "Can't you behave?" (p. 250)

Chapter XV:

Answers will vary, however, the Deltas' denseness and total lack of understanding of what John wants to tell them should be expressed. Also, the fear of being deprived of *soma* should be reflected in the text.

Chapter XVI:

1. wrong	2. right	3. right	4. wrong	
5. right	6. wrong	7. right	8. right	9. wrong

Lösungen zu Worksheet 9:

Chapter XVII:

Correct statements:
1. – C. 2. – A. 3. – B. 4. – C. 5. – B. 6. – A.

Chapter XVIII:

Answers will vary.

Notizen:

Component 2: *Brave New World –* a Dystopian Novel of the 30's

2.1 Dystopia

Als Einstieg in diesen *Component* werden zunächst die ersten drei *Worksheets* aus *Component 1* gemeinsam besprochen.
Da die Schülerinnen und Schüler den Roman bereits gelesen haben, kann man mit einem *Brainstorming* in die Besprechung der Lektüre einsteigen, wodurch eine Mitbestimmung der Schülerinnen und Schüler über die in den nächsten Wochen zu besprechenden Themen erreicht wird. Es wird sicherlich in den meisten Kursen zu den im Folgenden aufgeführten und erarbeiteten Fragestellungen kommen.

Having read the novel *Brave New World* in the past weeks, what would you think is worthwhile discussing?

cloning	→	genetic engineering – Dolly
conditioning	→	mass media – advertisements
clash of cultures	→	values – love, friendship, loyalty
drugs	→	soft drugs, hard drugs – legalize them!
literature	→	Why read Shakespeare?

Die Zusammenstellung dieser möglichen Diskussionsstoffe wird nicht ohne ein lebhaftes Unterrichtsgespräch erfolgen können, in dessen Verlauf bereits einige Aspekte des Romans angesprochen werden. Anstatt nur eine Sammlung vorzunehmen, kann man auch eine Hitliste der Themen erstellen lassen, die den Schülerinnen und Schülern am wichtigsten erscheinen.

Daraufhin sollten die Schülerinnen und Schüler sich mit dem Genre, zu dem *Brave New World* gehört, auseinander setzen, um dann zu erarbeiten, dass zu der Zeit, als Huxley seinen Roman schrieb, noch keinerlei wissenschaftlicher Fortschritt hinsichtlich möglicher Manipulationen am Genmaterial von Pflanzen, Tieren oder Menschen denkbar war. Eine anschließende Begriffsklärung von Science-Fiction, Utopie und Dystopie runden diese Einführung ab. Obwohl Huxleys Roman durch die neueren naturwissenschaftlichen Erkenntnisse und Entwicklungen ungeahnt aktuell geworden ist, sollte man nicht auf Details der Genmanipulation, die im Übrigen kaum jemand ohne entsprechendes Studium wirklich verstehen wird, eingehen.

Considering the year of publication of *Brave New World*, namely 1932, what do you think Huxley's peers thought of his new world?

Nobody could possibly have believed back then that genetic engineering was possible and so everybody took the novel as a fictional portrayal of a horrible future state. Nowadays, his visions have acquired an air of possibility, which makes reading his book even more eerie.

Als Hausaufgabe sollen die folgenden drei Begriffe erklärt werden: Science-Fiction, Utopie, Dystopie. Als Alternative kann man auch die im Folgenden aufgeführten Definitionen kopieren und die Schülerinnen und Schüler erarbeiten lassen, zu welchem Genre *Brave New World* gehört.

With the help of a dictionary and the Internet explain the following words: science-fiction, utopia, dystopia.

science-fiction	Genre of fiction with an imaginary scientific or technological basis. Science-fiction usually takes its ideas from current ideas in society and thus tries to make its audience aware of certain problems in society. The term science-fiction was coined in 1927 by Hugo Gernsback. Prominent authors of science-fiction are Jules Verne, H. G. Wells, Isaac Asimov and Arthur C. Clarke. However, a number of other mainstream authors have also contributed to this genre such as Doris Lessing and George Orwell.
utopia	The term utopia comes from Greek and means "no place". Thomas More described an ideal state in his book *Utopia* in 1516 and that coined the name of the genre. Plato's *Republic* is another well-known example of a utopian book. Utopias are a common subject in science-fiction.
dystopia	A dystopia is an imaginary society whose evil qualities are meant to serve as a moral or political warning. In the 19th century, Jules Verne and H. G. Wells described dystopias in their science-fiction novels. Examples of dystopian novels in the 20th century are George Orwell's *1984*, Ray Bradbury's *Fahrenheit 451* and Anthony Burgess' *A Clockwork Orange*.

Da das Genre Science-Fiction nicht nur durch Romane abgedeckt wird, sondern auch viele Filme die möglichen Entwicklungen der Menschheit unter Berücksichtigung der immer weiter fortschreitenden Möglichkeiten von Technologie und Genmanipulation zum Thema haben, bietet es sich an, hierüber mit dem Kurs ein Gespräch zu führen. Um Unterschiede zwischen Buch und Film zu verdeutlichen, soll später die allerdings eher misslungene Verfilmung von *Brave New World* in Ausschnitten behandelt werden. Darüber hinaus bietet es sich auch an, eine recht gelungene Verfilmung einer Dystopie zu berücksichtigen. So könnte etwa der Film *Gattaca* (1998, USA, Andrew Niccol) von einer kleinen Gruppe von Schülerinnen und Schülern vorgestellt werden. Auch Filme wie *Twelve Monkeys* (1995, USA, Terry Gilliam), *Das fünfte Element* (1997, USA, Luc Besson), *Matrix* (1999, USA, Andy and Larry Wachowski), *Equilibrium* (2002, USA, Kurt Wimmer) oder auch aus deutscher Produktion *Blueprint* (2003, D, Rolf Schübel) können Grundlage für eine solche Präsentation sein. Für die Vorbereitung der Präsentation ist es nicht zwingend nötig, dass die Gruppen diese Filme auf Englisch sehen.
Vorab sollte man allerdings mit dem Kurs erarbeiten, worauf es bei einer solchen Präsentation ankommt.

How to Present a Film

The aim of presenting a film in class is basically to convey to your audience the answers you found to the following questions:

- What is presented in the movie?
- How is it presented?
- What does it mean?

To make it a successful and enjoyable experience for both the audience and yourself as the presenter, you should make your presentation understandable (contents) and illustrate your statements for your classmates.

1. General conditions

- You have 20 – 25 minutes for your presentation
- The following equipment is available: DVD-player, video recorder, overhead projector, CD player, board, walls for posters.
- Use formal language.
- Give vocabulary explanations if necessary, but do not use too many unknown words.
- Use quotes from the film or from interviews to make your points clear.
- Use stills from the movie to illustrate your points.
- Prepare handouts with the most important information from your presentation.

2. Preparing a presentation

- Define your topic precisely.
- Use different sources to find information on your topic: the Internet, magazines, newspapers, encyclopedias, dictionaries, etc.
- Check the quality of your sources.
- Scan the chosen texts for useful information and make notes.
- Reduce the information gathered to those points that can clearly help to explain what you want to reveal about the movie.
- Illustrate your ideas in a mind-map.
- Give your presentation a structure:
  <u>Introduction:</u>
  – State the basic information about your movie (title, genre, director, actors, date of release, scriptwriter, theme).
  – Give background information to your film (e.g. Is it based on a novel or real event? What difficulties did the director and producer have to face? Why did the actors accept the role?).

Main part:
- Write a one-page synopsis of what happens in your film.
- Choose 3 – 5 key scenes that you think are important to explain your topic.
- Inform about the following aspects for each scene: the context of the scene within the movie, reasons for your choice, development and solution of the problems in the scene and the impact on the characters. Relevant aspects of acting, camera operations, editing, lighting, soundtrack, special effects, colours, etc.

Conclusion:
- Put the film into its wider context.
- Discuss the problem the movie presents and relate it to other movies, fictional texts, non-fictional texts or works of art.
- Summarize your ideas briefly.

Practise your presentation.

3. Giving a presentation

- Speak clearly and make short pauses.
- Use your notes only from time to time to reassure yourself of your structure. Do not simply read from your written text.
- Maintain eye-contact with your audience.
- Use visual material to illustrate your points:
  the key scenes of your movie, stills, film posters, transparencies or handouts with key words or your mind-map etc.
- Only present information that you have fully understood.
- Give your audience the chance to ask questions and discuss their impressions.
- Thank your audience for listening.
- Ask for feedback (evaluation) of your presentation.

2.2 Let's talk to the experts

Um den Schülerinnen und Schülern einen Einblick in die Vielfalt der Probleme und Chancen, die die Entwicklung der Genmanipulation bietet, zu gewähren, kann man ihnen die folgenden Sachtexte präsentieren. Da eine Erarbeitung der fünf Texte in der gesamten Klasse etwas zu zeitaufwändig wäre, bietet sich hier die Form des Expertenpuzzles an. Dies erfordert eine sorgfältige Vorbereitung. Die Durchführung soll im Folgenden kurz skizziert werden.

- Die fünf Texte werden auf farbiges Papier kopiert, wobei jedem Text eine Farbe zugeordnet wird. Dies erleichtert bei der Arbeit die schnelle Zuordnung der Schülerinnen und Schüler zu ihren Gruppen.
- Es werden sechs Gruppen zu je fünf Schülerinnen und Schülern gebildet. Jedes Mitglied einer Gruppe erhält einen der fünf Texte.
- Die Aufgabe besteht darin, den Text aufmerksam zu lesen und dann den anderen Mitgliedern der Gruppe kurz Bericht über den Inhalt zu erstatten.
- In einer zweiten Runde werden die Gruppen neu gemischt, sodass alle Schülerinnen und Schüler, die denselben Text gelesen haben, nun zusammenarbeiten. Sie fertigen gemeinsam eine Zusammenfassung an.
- Nun gehen die Schülerinnen und Schüler in die ursprünglichen Gruppen zurück und berichten den anderen Mitgliedern ausführlich über ihren Text.
- Der abschließende Test gibt Auskunft darüber, wie gut die Schülerinnen und Schüler ihre Gruppen über ihre Texte informiert haben.

Die Gruppeneinteilung kann entweder zufällig erfolgen oder man lässt die Klasse selbst die Gruppen bilden oder man weist einzelne Schülerinnen und Schüler einzelnen Texten zu, die in der Länge variieren und daher binnendifferenziert einsetzbar sind. Der erste Text (*Blood Cells Turn Cancer Killers*) ist deutlich kürzer als die übrigen vier Texte; falls man keine schwächeren Schülerinnen und Schüler im Kurs hat, kann man ihn weglassen und muss dann entsprechend die Anzahl der Gruppen und *Worksheet 11* abändern.

Notizen:

Blood Cells Turn Cancer Killers

Scientists in Greater Manchester have come up with a technique to modify white blood cells so they destroy cancerous tumours.

The researchers at the Paterson Institute in Manchester have used genetic engineering to modify the blood cells, it was revealed on Tuesday.

Backed by Cancer Research UK, the researchers plan to start the first patient trial of the treatment in the UK next year.

They say the power of the human immune system has been harnessed to tackle cancers, which are not normally eliminated because the body actually produces them.

During the research white blood cells were modified, enabling the body to recognise and attack the cancer cells.

Professor Robert Hawkins, from Cancer Research UK's Department of Medical Oncology, said the immune system can get "confused" by cancer.

He said: "What we've done in this new study is give our immune cells the equipment they need to recognize, home in on and destroy cells from tumours.

We've shown that the technique works 100% of the time in the laboratory, but the real test will be whether it works in cancer patients, which we'll begin to look at in the clinical trial."

The researchers sought to overcome the "cancer confusion" problem by tweaking the DNA in white blood cells.

They took blood samples from 10 patients with advanced bowel cancer and extracted white blood cells, called T-lymphocytes.

The lymphocytes were modified by fusing a "homing" gene that specifically targets bowel cancer cells with a "kill" gene that causes the white cells to launch an attack.

Experiments were carried out to test the engineered lymphocytes in targeting bowel cancer. Results showed cells from all patients showed powerful anti-cancer activity.

The trial is due to take place next year at Manchester's Christie Hospital. *(296 words)*

http://newsvote.bbc.co.uk/mpapps/pagetools/print/news.bbc.co.uk./1/hi/england/2907881.stm

to harness here: to control, to make use of

to home in on to aim for

to tweak to change slightly, especially in order to make more correct, effective or suitable

to launch to begin or introduce

How to Live Longer

This year's Reith lecturer, Professor Tom Kirkwood, claims ageing is "neither inevitable nor necessary" and invites us to "prepare for the longevity revolution". While, as he states, we are not programmed to die, it is also true that our genes have not been designed for long life.

Most of our ancestors were hunter-gathers who led short and brutal lives before falling prey to disease, starvation, predators or competitors. Their genes evolved to inhabit bodies for just a couple of decades before being passed on to their offspring.

The fat of the bodies left behind was of little concern to genes that had already fled into the next generation. Defects that showed up only in later years, leading to cancer, heart disease, Alzheimer's or stroke, would have escaped the attentions of natural selection. Longterm maintenance and repair was never a priority.

Our genes haven't changed. They are still designed for the short term, no matter how carefully we maintain and service our bodies. Ageing is a genetic disease. To cure it, we will need to turn shortterm genes into longterm genes and this will be accomplished only by genetic engineering and gene therapy.

Ever since the first microbe crawled out of the primordial soup, Mother Nature has operated a strict policy of breeding from only the fit and healthy. The vast majority of creatures born into this world have departed from it without leaving any descendants. For many it might have been just bad luck, but others inherited bad genes that led to illness, frailty or plain lack of sex appeal.

Darwin described this motor of evolution but lamented its "clumsy, wasteful, blundering, low and horribly cruel" action. His cousin Francis Galton and others proposed to replace human natural selection with breeding programmes to "improve the racial qualities of future generations".

This "eugenics" movement was openly racist with the aim of ensuring that the "feeble nations" give way before the "nobler varieties of mankind".

In Germany, the 1934 racial hygiene law led to enforced sterilisation of more than 80,000 people considered "unworthy". US eugenics policies between 1907 and 1960 resulted in the enforced sterilisation of at least 60,000 individuals. Even in liberal Sweden, more than 62,000 people (mostly women) with handicaps or considered "undesirable", were sterilised against their will.

With such a terrible history, it is perhaps not surprising that many fear the human genome will become a eugenicist's toolkit. But there is a huge difference. Whereas eugenics seeks to restrict fertility by enforced or coerced sterilisation, gene therapy seeks simply to correct gene defects that make us sick.

to fall prey to to receive bad treatment by sb or sth

offspring a person's children

to maintain to keep in good condition

primordial existing at or since the beginning of the world

eugenics the study of methods of improving humans by allowing only carefully chosen people to reproduce

toolkit set of tools

to coerce to persuade sb forcefully to do sth which they are unwilling to do

The aim is not to produce Galton's "highly bred human race" but to eliminate genes that cause disease including the infirmities of old age.

Just as vaccines have conquered smallpox, gene therapy may eliminate genetic diseases like cystic fibrosis and muscular dystrophy and eventually, the most common of them all, the ageing process.

Hardly a day goes by without Prince Charles warning us of the dangers of genetic engineering. Yet the human genome has revealed that nature is the busiest genetic engineer. More than 200 of our genes appear to have been captured from bacteria and much of the rest of the genome is a junkyard filled with the corpses of retrovirus and other parasites that have been hopping in and out of our chromosomes for millennia.

Comparing our chromosomes to those of other species, we can see that in addition to inserting new genes, nature has reshuffled, duplicated and deleted large settlements of our chromosomes making about one major rearrangement every million years.

So if nature is not averse to a bit of genetic tinkering, why should we be so wary? With the decline of religion, the genome seems to have emerged as the secular equivalent of the soul: genes are sacred. Yet DNA is not spiritual. DNA comes out of your cells looking like strands of slimy cotton. You can store it in the freezer, post it to your friends; you can even eat it without suffering any ethical crisis. Genes are just bits of us and gene therapy is just another form of medicine. Fixing a broken arm is not considered to interfere with God's plan so why should fixing a broken gene be any different?

Of course any technology can be abused. But anyone wishing to use the human genome to make a super race would not know where to start. Identifying those genes whose defects cause disease is a difficult enough task; unravelling the genetic and environmental interactions that lead to complex characters like good looks, physical strength or intelligence is far harder.

It would be foolish to by-pass the potential benefits of gene therapy because of unreasonable fears of its misuse. A surgeon could stab us in the heart but we trust him not to: we don't ban scalpels from operating theatres.

If we really wish to banish genetic diseases, including the ageing process, then we must overcome our fears of dabbling in our own genome. *(834 words)*

vaccine *Impfung*
smallpox *Pocken*

to tinker to make small changes to sth in a way that is not decisive, in an attempt to repair or improve it
wary not completely trusting or certain about sth
secular not having any connection with religion
to interfere to involve yourself in matters which are connected with other people when your involvement is neither wanted nor helpful

to dabble to take a slight and not very serious interest in a subject or try a particular activity for a short period

Pope Expresses Opposition to GMOs, Cites Need for "the Respect of Nature"

GMO genetically modified organism

In a call that could have an impact on farming techniques in predominantly Catholic parts of the developing world, Pope John Paul II said that using genetically modified organisms to increase production was contrary to God's will.

Speaking Nov. 12 to an estimated 50,000 farmers from Italy and elsewhere at a special outdoor mass dedicated to farmers, the Pope told them and their colleagues worldwide to "resist the temptation of high productivity and profit that word to the detriment of the respect of nature." The pontiff added that "when (farmers) forget this basic principle and become tyrants of the earth rather than its custodians... sooner or later the earth rebels."

detriment harm or damage
pontiff Pope

Furthermore, the Pope said, if modern farming techniques "don't reconcile themselves with the simple language of nature in a healthy balance, the life of man will run even greater risks, of which already we are seeing worrying signs." He did not specify the signs.

to reconcile to find a way in which two situations that are opposed to each other are in agreement

Though experts said that the impact of the Pope's statement on farming were likely to have a limited impact in developed countries, where attitudes toward biotechnology were already well developed, the comments could have an influence in the developing world.

Heart Turner, a Rome food safety consultant formerly associated with the World Food Programme and the Italian Ministry of Agriculture, said that the new point of view from the Holy See could mold attitudes in Catholic regions such as Latin America and parts of Africa. "In many parts of the world, the Pope's views on a wide variety of subjects are taken far more seriously than their own government's views of the results of any scientific survey," Turner told BNA on Nov. 13.

Holy See government of the Roman Catholic Church under the Pope

BNA Bureau of National Affairs (Washington)

The statements apparently represent a change for the Vatican, which had previously said it was not opposed to some forms of biotechnology if the science helped feed poor countries and was not misused. When contacted by BNA on Nov. 14, a spokesman for the Vatican declined to elaborate on John Paul II's statements.

Helping opponents? John Monyo, the head of the biotechnology section at the United Nation's Rome-based Food and Agriculture Organization, told BNA on Nov. 14 that the statements could give ammunition to secular groups opposed to bioengineering.

secular not having any connection with religion

"The impact of something like this is very difficult to estimate, but I would not be surprised to find the statements being used to support the views of non-religious groups," Monyo said. "Groups already opposed to genetically-altered products will now be able to say that even the Pope supports their views."

Italy's Green Party, which has long opposed the use of genetically modified organisms in Italy and elsewhere, issued a short statement dated Nov. 14 applauding the Pope's statements.

But in Italy itself, the impact is expected to be minimal since the country is already one of the most conservative countries in Europe in terms of GMOs. Prime Minister Giuliano Amato has repeatedly acted to tighten restrictions on the use of genetically altered food products, and the moves so far seemed backed by public opinion. In August, for example, Italy banned four kinds of genetically modified corn and then refused to eliminate the ban a month later when the European Union said the corn was safe. That case is on hold pending a decision whether an EU member state has the right to impose stricter standards than those from the EU even when there is no published evidence that the products may be harmful.

The FAO's Monyo said it was important that statements from the Vatican not affect the policies of world governments. "One thing most experts agree on is that government policy should be secular," he said. "Individuals can believe what they choose and be influenced by who they choose, but it is important governments stay clear of adopting views (only because they are) put forth by one religion or another."

A spokesman for the Italian Ministry of Agriculture, which already takes a generally anti-GMO stance on most issues, told BNA on Nov. 14 that it had no plans to adjust its policies as a result of the Pope's statements. An official with the testing division at the University of Bologna, which tests privately-developed GMOs for safety, also said that the comments would have no impact on the group's activities.

The Nov. 12 religious service for farmers is part of special Holy Year activities called for by John Paul to mark the start of Christianity's third millennium. A wide variety of professions have had special religious services held in their honor at the Vatican City. *(766 words)*

FAO Food and Agriculture Organization

stance a way of thinking about sth

Eric Leyman (Copyright 2000 by the Bureau of National Affairs, Inc., Washington);
www.netlink.de/gen/Zeitung/2000/001115a.html

We Must Not Clone Humans, Bush Tells the Senate

President George Bush made an impassioned plea for a total ban on human cloning yesterday after the Senate announced that it would hold a vote on the issue.

Mr Bush, whose opposition extends to embryonic cloning for medical research, made his plea at the White House meeting with opponents of the research, hours after the Senate majority leader, Tom Daschle, confirmed that a vote would be held within the next few weeks. With the pro and anti camps equally divided, the balance is held by about 20 undecided senators, at whom Mr Bush was directing his remarks yesterday.

"We must stop human cloning before it starts," the President declared. "We must ask ourselves what is right. Even the most noble ends do not always justify the means."

He endorsed the Republican-led Senate Bill demanding a ban, and stressed that he opposed not only reproductive cloning to create another human being, which is abhorred by most people including the scientific community, but also cloning to produce embryos from which stem cells could be extracted.

Many scientists support the latter, saying it could be vital in the search for cures to diseases such as cancer, diabetes and Parkinson's and Alzheimer's. "That's where the divide is," Mr Daschle, a supporter of research cloning, said.

Almost simultaneously, a group of 40 Nobel prize-winning scientists issued a declaration supporting research cloning, arguing that an across-the-board ban "would have a chilling effect on all scientific research in the United States."

A ban, they said, would be "unprecedented and ill-conceived", placing medical research and development in the United States at a dangerous disadvantage with foreign competitors.

But Mr Bush was having none of this. "Life is a creation, not a commodity", he said. "Our children are not products to be designed and manufactured." Conjuring up a nightmarish vision of a world in which "human beings are grown to provide spare body parts", the President said that whatever the technical distinction between reproductive cloning and research cloning, in practice it would be impossible to enforce. Even stem cell research using embryos would "require the destruction of nascent human life", he said.

In words which will delight anti-abortionists and the social conservatives who are an important part of his political base, Mr Bush spoke of the "fundamental principle that no human life should be exploited or extinguished for the benefit of another".

President Bush's attitude towards cloning has, if anything, hardened since last August when he gave grudging approval to federal funding for research on existing human stem cell lines. Yesterday he called

to endorse to make a public statement of your approval or support for sth or sb

ill-conceived badly planned or unwise

commodity a substance or product that can be traded, bought or sold

to conjure to make sth appear as if by magic

nascent small because only recently formed or started but likely to grow larger quickly

grudging a grudging action or feeling is one which you do or have unwillingly

for more support for the research, which, he said, did not involve the destruction of human life.

A bipartisan Bill outlawing cloning has already been overwhelmingly passed by the House of Representatives. In the Senate, advocates of a ban have been heartened by the support of Bill Frist of Tennessee, the lone doctor in the Senate and an influential voice on medical issues, who has come round in support of President Bush.

Their cause has also been helped by an unconfirmed report that the controversial Italian fertility doctor Severino Antinori has successfully established a cloned pregnancy, now in its eighth week.

The claim, which was made last week in the Gulf News has been widely discounted in America, but the very thought of it has heightened alarm ahead of the vote. *(564 words)*

We Must Not Clone Humans – Rupert Cornwell
THE INDEPENDENT, 14.11.2002

bipartisan supported by or consisting of two political parties

to discount to decide that sth or sb is not worth consideration or attention

Dolly the Sheep Is Put to Sleep, Aged Only Six

Premature ageing and disease cast doubt over the future for cloning animals.

She was a copy. And, like most copies, she faded a little bit quicker than the original.

Dolly, the sheep, the world's first animal to be cloned from an adult cell, has been put to sleep, it was announced yesterday. She was only six and a half years old – barely 40 in human terms. Already being treated for arthritis, Dolly was found to be suffering from a progressive lung disease.

Legally, she was an experimental research animal, and as such it fell to the man who created her, Ian Wilmut – holder of the cloning project research licence at the Roslin Institute near Edinburgh – to make the final decision to put her painlessly to death.

Last year, in the wake of the arthritis announcement, he told the Guardian that, had he been a hill farmer and Dolly an ordinary sheep, he would already have had her put down.

The premature death of Dolly supports the views of scientists in Japan and the US who maintain that all cloned animals are born with health problems.

Roslin spokesman Harry Griffin, probably the nearest thing Dolly ever had to an agent, was cautious on the significance of the ewe's death. "Sheep can live to 11 or 12 years," he said. "Lung infections are common in older sheep, particularly those housed inside. A full post-mortem is being conducted and we will report any significant findings."

After the post-mortem examination, Dolly will be stuffed and put on display at the National Museum of Scotland.

Dolly was born on July 5 1996, from three mothers: one ewe to provide the DNA, another to provide the egg into which the DNA was injected, and a third to carry the resulting cloned embryo to term.

Dolly's genetic mother (the DNA was taken from an udder cell, and her name was a reference to Dolly Parton) was six when she was cloned. This may mean that the real age of clones is their age since birth, plus the age of the genetic donor.

The revelation to the world of Dolly's existence, in 1997, was the scientific sensation of the decade. Scientific orthodoxy declared that cloning was impossible: here was the living, bleating and woolly proof.

A frenzy of speculation followed about what cloning could achieve. But we now know that cloning is difficult, expensive, and dangerous for the animals involved. Bill Clinton was fascinated by cloning, but George Bush is repelled by it and wants to ban human cloning, even for medical research. Claims of cloned humans by space alien lovers and a shrill Italian fertility doctor remain unproven.

in the wake of if sth happens in the wake of sth else, it happens after and often because of it

to maintain to express firmly your belief that sth is true

ewe adult female sheep

to repel to make you not want to be near, see or think about sth; to cause disgust

"We must await the results of the post-mortem on Dolly in order to assess whether her relatively premature death was in any way connected with the fact that she was a clone," said Professor Richard Gardner, chairman of the Royal Society working group on stem cell research and therapeutic cloning. "If there is a link, it will provide further evidence of the dangers inherent in reproductive cloning and the irresponsibility of anybody who is trying to extend such work to humans."

Dolly is survived by six uncloned lambs. *(539 words)*

to assess to judge or decide the amount, value, quality or importance of; to evaluate

inherent existing as a natural or basic part of sth

Nach Abschluss dieser Gruppenarbeit, die nicht mehr als zwei Doppelstunden in Anspruch nehmen sollte, wird dem Kurs folgender Test vorgelegt *(Worksheet 10)*, der in 15 bis 20 Minuten ausgefüllt werden kann.

Lösungen zu Worksheet 10:

Text S. 43: Blood Cells Turn Cancer Killers

1. wrong
2. right

Genetic engineering is viewed as a means to help doctors cure cancer.

Text S. 44f.: How to Live Longer

1. right
2. wrong
3. right
4. wrong

eugenics: aims to restrict fertility by enforced sterilisation
gene therapy: aims to correct gene defects

Text S. 46f.: Pope Expresses Opposition to GMOs

1. wrong
2. right
3. right
4. wrong

The Pope is very much against any kind of genetic engineering.

Text S. 48f.: We Must Not Clone Humans

1. right
2. wrong

President Bush is totally against any kind of genetic engineering.

Text S. 50f.: Dolly the Sheep Is Put to Sleep, Aged Only Six

1. wrong
2. right

It seems as if clones are not as healthy as naturally-born animals. They age and die prematurely.

Das auswertende Gespräch bietet Raum für Verständnisfragen oder Diskussionen im Plenum über das Gelesene. Eine solche Diskussion sollte nicht über eine Unterrichtsstunde hinausgehen, da das Thema in seiner ganzen Komplexität sicherlich nicht erschöpfend behandelt werden kann.

Notizen:

Genetic engineering – what you remember from the texts:

Text: Blood Cells Turn Cancer Killers
Right or wrong?
1. Scientists in the UK have developed a method to use red blood cells to kill cancerous cells.
2. The method works 100 % of the time in the laboratory.

How does the author view genetic engineering in this text?

Text: How to Live Longer
Right or wrong?
1. Ageing is a genetic disease.
2. Darwin's cousin wanted to strengthen people's genes by letting them breed as they wanted.
3. Many countries sterilized individuals with handicaps.
4. According to this text, gene therapy is a horrible thing.

What is the difference between eugenics and gene therapy?

Text: Pope Expresses Opposition to GMOs
Right or wrong?
1. The Pope thinks using GMOs is in accordance with God's will.
2. The Pope's comments could have an influence on the developing world.
3. Italy's Green Party is happy about the Pope's speech.
4. Governments should listen to the Pope and found their decisions on what he says.

What is the Pope's view on genetic engineering?

Text: We Must Not Clone Humans
Right or wrong?
1. President Bush is totally against genetic engineering.
2. Scientists all over the world have also declared that they are against any research on genetic engineering.

What is President Bush's view on genetic engineering?

Text: Dolly the Sheep Is Put to Sleep, Aged Only Six
Right or wrong?
1. Dolly was put down because she was suffering from old age.
2. Dolly was living proof that cloning is possible.

Which health problems are obviously connected with cloning?

Component 3: Behavioural Engineering

Vor dem Einstieg in die Arbeit mit *Component 3* sollten die *Worksheets 4–6* aus *Component 1* besprochen werden.

Nachdem die Gentechnologie als Mittel der vorgeburtlichen Einflussnahme näher betrachtet wurde, sollen im Folgenden die Möglichkeiten der Konditionierung und der „Hypnopädie“ als weitere Manipulationsinstrumente des Staates untersucht werden. Dazu sollen die Schülerinnen und Schüler das zweite Kapitel des Romans erneut lesen und dessen Inhalt kurz zusammenfassen. Darüber hinaus sollte eine Schülerin oder ein Schüler zu dieser Stunde Informationen zu Pavlov zusammentragen, ohne jedoch auf seine Versuche einzugehen.

We have found out that genetic engineering is practised systematically in *Brave New World* to produce the required quantity and quality of human beings for the World State. Name some other means that are used to create the types of *people* that this society needs, that is, those that can be counted on to give no trouble to their supervisors.

Answer: conditioning, hypnopaedia

Zur Vergegenwärtigung des Inhalts trägt ein(e) Schüler(in) die als Hausaufgabe zu dieser Stunde angefertigte Zusammenfassung von Kapitel II des Romans vor, die in etwa folgendermaßen aussieht:

Summary of chapter II

The Director leads the students into the Neo-Pavlovian Conditioning Room where they are shown how Delta-babies are trained to hate books and flowers by combining the sight and touch of books and flowers with noise and electric shocks. They are told that the Deltas are not supposed to read books because reading could give them undesirable ideas and that the State's economic policy does not accept the enjoyment of pure nature because it is free of cost and the people are meant to consume. Then the Director demonstrates how children are indoctrinated to love their living conditions through sleep-teaching.

Notizen:

3.1 Classical conditioning

Anschließend informiert eine Schülerin/ein Schüler kurz über Ivan Pavlov. Die wichtigsten Informationen werden (von einem Schüler) an der Tafel festgehalten.

Ivan Petrovich Pavlov

- 1849–1936
- Russian scientist (physiologist)
- most famous experiment: "Pavlovian Dog"
- discovery of the "conditioned reflex" (reaction to a stimulus that would normally not be elicited)
- classical conditioning

Durch die Beantwortung der *while-reading-Aufgaben* zu Kapitel II (s. *Component 1*) sind die Schülerinnen und Schüler grundsätzlich schon mit den Verfahren der „Erziehung" in *Brave New World* bekannt. In *Component 3* geht es hauptsächlich darum, ein tieferes Verständnis der Idee durch Heranziehen der behavioristischen Verhaltenstheorie zu erlangen und eine Interpretation einer Szene in Form eines Storyboards für einen möglichen Film zu versuchen, die anschließend mit der tatsächlichen Umsetzung (bzw. Auslassung) in dem Film *Brave New World* von Leslie Libman und Larry Williams verglichen werden kann.

Nachdem Ivan Pavlov schon kurz vorgestellt wurde, soll die Methode des *classical conditioning* durch Lesen des Textes aus einer Online-Enzyklopädie (*Kopiervorlage S. 56*) mit dem Arbeitsauftrag, die Hauptaussagen grafisch unterstützt darzustellen, verdeutlicht werden. Anschließend sollen die Ergebnisse auf die Darbietung der klassischen Konditionierung im zweiten Kapitel des Romans übertragen werden.

1. Point out the main statements of the text and present them by also making use of simple visualization techniques.
2. Describe the conditioning of the babies demonstrated in chapter II in terms of classical conditioning and add the World State's aim.

Die Ergebnisse könnten auf Folie oder an der Tafel präsentiert werden und in etwa so aussehen:

Classical conditioning

unconditional stimulus: food	→	unconditional response: salivation
repeated combination of: tone + food	→	salivation
conditional stimulus: tone	→	conditional response: salivation

Classical Conditioning

Classical conditioning – also called *"pavlovian conditioning"* or *"respondent conditioning"* – involves learning about the association of two or more (usually external) stimuli. Classical conditioning is generally associated with Ivan Pavlov. When two things generally occur together, encountering one can bring the other to mind (c.f., Aristotle's *law of contiguity*). Thus, when Pavlov's dog hears the tone, salivation and other food-related responses occur because the tone and food commonly occurred together in the dog's experience.

In the most famous example of classical conditioning, Pavlov exposed dogs to repeated pairings of a tone and food. Again and again, a tone was audible for several seconds and then the dog was given a small portion of food. Before these pairings, the dog had innate, unconditional, food-related responses (most famously, salivation) to the food, but no food-related reactions to the tone. The food, therefore, was called an *unconditional stimulus* (abbreviated *US* or *UCS),* and salivation was called an *unconditional response* (abbreviated *UR* or *UCR).* These terms were chosen to reflect that no experience or *conditions* were needed for this stimulus-response relationship to occur. The food and tone were part of an *unconditional reflex.*

The tone, however, initially elicited no food-related responses, and was therefore termed a *neutral stimulus* (abbreviated *NS).* After the dog experienced the pairings of the tone and food, however, the effects of the tone were changed. The previously neutral tone began to elicit salivation. The newly conditioned tone, therefore, was called a *conditional stimulus* (abbreviated *CS*) because its effects on food-related responses were conditional upon the dog's experiences. The salivation elicited by the tone, also conditional upon the dog's experience, was called a *conditioned* (or *conditional*) *response* (abbreviated *CR).* After conditioning, the tone and salivation were part of a *conditional reflex.*

Extinction of a conditional reflex occurs when the conditional stimulus is repeatedly presented in the absence of the unconditional stimulus. Food-related responses to conditional stimulus generally cease over the course of extinction.

Classical conditioning is involved in a number of important phenomena, like taste aversions, phobias, sexual fetishes, immune function, drug tolerance, and drug overdose.

http://en.wikipedia.org/w/wiki.phtml?title=Conditioning&action=submit

Neo-Pavlovian conditioning (*Brave New World*, chapter II)

unconditional stimulus: flowers, books	→	unconditional response: joy
stimulus: flowers, books + siren, electric shock	→	conditional response: fear
conditional stimulus: flowers, books	→	conditional response: fear

Aim: Deltas will not want to read books.
Deltas will not enjoy nature.

3.2 Behaviourism

An dieser Stelle darf der Begriff des *behaviourism* nicht fehlen; er soll hier jedoch lediglich durch Einbringen des Artikels zu John B. Watson in der *Grolier Encyclopedia* und folgender Hausaufgabe gestreift werden. Bei den Themen Konditionierung und Behaviorismus können die Schülerinnen und Schüler sicher auf Wissen aus dem Biologie- und Pädagogikunterricht zurückgreifen, sodass eine Vertiefung nicht nötig ist.

Read the entry for John B. Watson from the Grolier's encyclopedia and mark the most important information.

In einem Unterrichtsgespräch werden zu Beginn der nächsten Stunde die Prinzipien der klassischen Konditionierung wiederholt, Grundgedanken der behavioristischen Verhaltenstheorie besprochen, kritisch beleuchtet und ein Bezug zu unserem täglichen Leben hergestellt.

An der Tafel könnte das Wichtigste folgendermaßen festgehalten werden:

behaviourism

field of study:	animal and human behaviour
idea:	behaviour can be explained in terms of stimulus and response
experiment:	substitution of stimulus and response
aim:	programming of man's reaction to certain things
spokesmen:	John B. Watson, F. B. Skinner
view of man:	behaviour and character are determined by the environment
danger:	man can be conditioned systematically
problem:	simplistic, superficial view of human nature; no consideration of man's inner activities (reason, mind, soul, consciousness, imagination)

John B. Watson

The psychologist John Broadus Watson, born Greenville, S.C., Jan. 9 1878, died Sept. 25 1958, was the principal spokesman for rigorous *behaviourism* during the formative years of American psychology.
Strongly influenced by mechanistic materialism in biology and neurology at the University of Chicago, where he received his doctorate in 1903, Watson shunned the prevailing methods and concerns of the then dominant school of introspectionism. He studied animal behaviour and described it in terms of two categories: stimulus and response. Later he borrowed the terminology of conditioning from the Russian reflexologists Vladimir Bekhterev and Ivan Pavlov.

In 1908, Watson was appointed professor at Johns Hopkins University, where he remained until 1920 when a scandal obliged him to resign. He worked subsequently in advertising. While at Johns Hopkins, Watson first experimented solely with animals but later (1918) extended his research and explanatory principles to behaviour in children and to behaviour modification. Throughout his career, Watson was a highly vocal advocate of extreme environmentalism, stressing the preponderant role of the milieu in determining behaviour and character. His major works include *Behaviour: An Introduction to Comparative Psychology* (1914) and *Psychology from the Standpoint of a Behaviourist* (1919).

from: Grolier Multimedia Encyclopedia, 1997

John B. Watson's biography tells us that he worked in the advertising business later in his life. What do you make of this fact?

The advertising industry makes use of the techniques of conditioning. In order to sell their products they frequently combine two things (the product + something attractive for the target group) to provoke a reaction in the consumer (buy the product) that the product alone would not have elicited (conditioned response).

Can you name some examples?

For example, beer is often presented with beautiful young girls in bikinis.

Um die Schülerinnen und Schüler zu detailliertem Lesen des Textes und einer Interpretation anzuregen, erhalten sie die Aufgabe, in Partnerarbeit die Szene, in der die klassische Konditionierung beschrieben wird (S. 40, Z. 22 – S. 42, Z. 11) zu visualisieren, indem sie ein *storyboard* für einen möglichen Film entwerfen. Falls nötig, sollte kurz erklärt werden, dass die einzelnen Kästchen der Kopiervorlage mit groben Zeichnungen des umzusetzenden Textes gefüllt werden. Darunter ist Platz für knappe Hinweise zur Arbeit der Kamera und eventuell gesprochenen Text. Es ist davon auszugehen, dass die Schülerinnen und Schüler mit Grundbegriffen der Kameraarbeit vertraut sind; hilfreich wäre aber wahrscheinlich eine Kopie einer Übersicht, die in jedem neuen Oberstufenlehrwerk zu finden ist.

Work with a partner and visualize the conditioning scene (p. 40, l. 22 – p. 42, l. 11) in the form of a storyboard for a film.

- Read the text carefully.
- Decide on the number of pictures you will need and give each picture a number.
- Illustrate your ideas in rough sketches.
- Where appropriate, give the cameraman information on field size, camera angle, camera movement, camera position.
- Add the spoken dialogue where necessary.
- You may use arrows etc. to make your ideas clearer.
- Be prepared to present your storyboard to the class.

Anschließend präsentieren die Partner ihre *storyboards*, die von dem Rest des Kurses kommentiert werden.
Nun werden die entsprechenden Stellen des Films (Szene 2 – 4, vgl. Szenenfolge S. 65) angeschaut und die Schülerinnen und Schüler stellen fest, dass die Regisseure sich entschlossen haben, diese Szene des Romans nicht in den Film aufzunehmen. Der Kurs macht sich Gedanken über mögliche Gründe.

Watch the corresponding film scene and compare it to your ideas as well as to the text.
Can you think of any reasons why the directors decided not to film the conditioning scene?

Als Hausaufgabe bietet es sich an, die Ergebnisse dieses Gesprächs zu verschriftlichen.

Write a comment on the fact that the directors of the film left out the conditioning scene.

3.3 Hypnopaedia

Die nächste Stunde soll nach dem Vortragen einiger Hausaufgaben mit einem kleinen Experiment beginnen, das den Schülerinnen und Schülern das Thema der „Hypnopädie" näher bringen soll. Die Lehrperson (oder ein eingeweihter Schüler oder noch besser ein vorbereiteter Tonträger) trägt mit ruhiger, sanfter, suggestiver Stimme einfache Sätze wiederholt vor, die Schülerinnen und Schüler hören ganz entspannt zu. Eine Unterstützung durch entspannende Musik wäre hilfreich. Folgender Text soll als kleine Anregung für eine mögliche Umsetzung gelten.

Are you ready to participate in an experiment? OK, relax. Close your eyes and listen.

Brave New World is a fascinating novel.
I really enjoy reading it.
Huxley's ideas are so interesting.
It's the best book I've ever read.
John B. Watson describes human behaviour in terms of stimulus and response.
That view is far too superficial.
Behaviourism is a very bad psychological theory because it denies the influence of the human soul and mind.
Behaviourists are superficial and materialistic.

Wake up now. Open your eyes.
Can you determine the "teaching method" that you have just experienced?

Nach dieser Erfahrung sollen die Ziele, die der Weltstaat mit dem Einsatz der „Hypnopädie" verfolgt, herausgefiltert werden, indem die Schülerinnen und Schüler in Einzelarbeit die Stellen im Text markieren, die darüber Auskunft geben. Die Ergebnisse werden an der Tafel gesammelt.

Read the passage about hypnopaedia (p. 45, l. 12 – p. 52, l. 3) again and mark all the parts that give us information about the aims of this teaching method in the *„Brave New World"*.

hypnopaedia

- moral education: not rational, no science (p. 48, ll. 30f.)
- lessons in elementary sex (p. 49, l. 21)
- lessons in elementary class consciousness (p. 49, ll. 21f.)
- inculcate more complex courses of behaviour (p. 51, ll. 3f.)
- "The greatest moralizing and socializing farce of all times." (p. 51, ll. 7f.)
- "Till at last the child's mind *is* these suggestions, and the sum of the suggestions *is* the child's mind. And not the child's mind only. The adult's mind too – all his life long. [...] But all these suggestions are *our* suggestions!" [...] "Suggestions from the State." (p. 51, ll. 20 – 26)

Storyboard

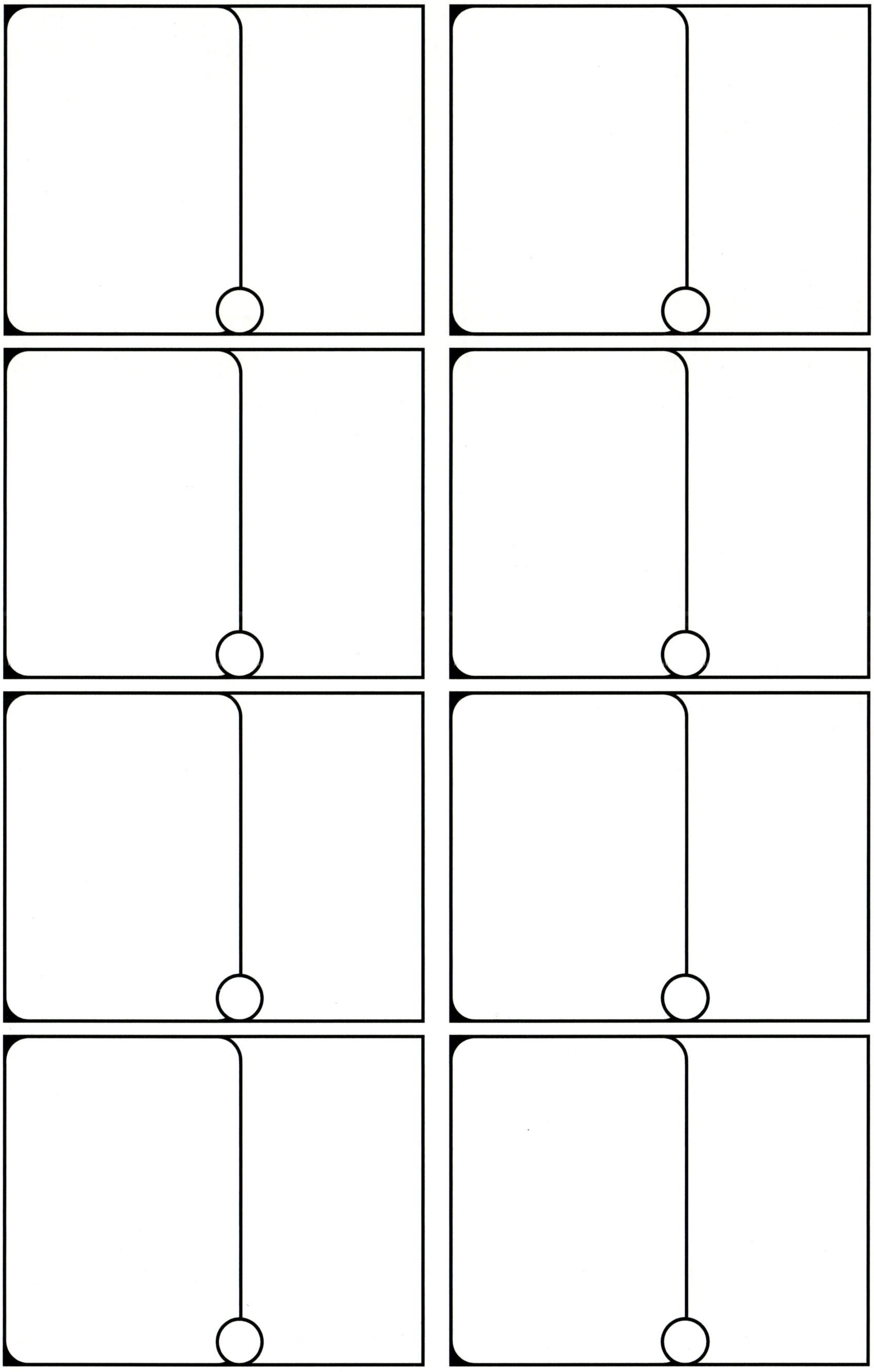

Lösungsvorschlag zur Kopiervorlage S. 61:

Um das themenspezifische Vokabular anzuwenden und die Paraphrasierungs- und Semantisierungstechniken der Schülerinnen und Schüler zu schulen, bietet sich das Verfahren eines *Half a Crossword* an, bei dem jede Schülerin/jeder Schüler eine Hälfte eines Kreuzworträtsels erhält *(Worksheets 11a und 11b)*. In Partnerarbeit erklären sie sich abwechselnd die einzusetzenden Wörter, ohne diese zu nennen.

Half a crossword: "hypnopaedia" A

Work with a partner. Without using the word in question, your partner will give you an explanation for the words for numbers 7 and 13 – 21 (down) and you will write them down. You will explain your words (numbers 1–12, across) for your partner. Take turns.

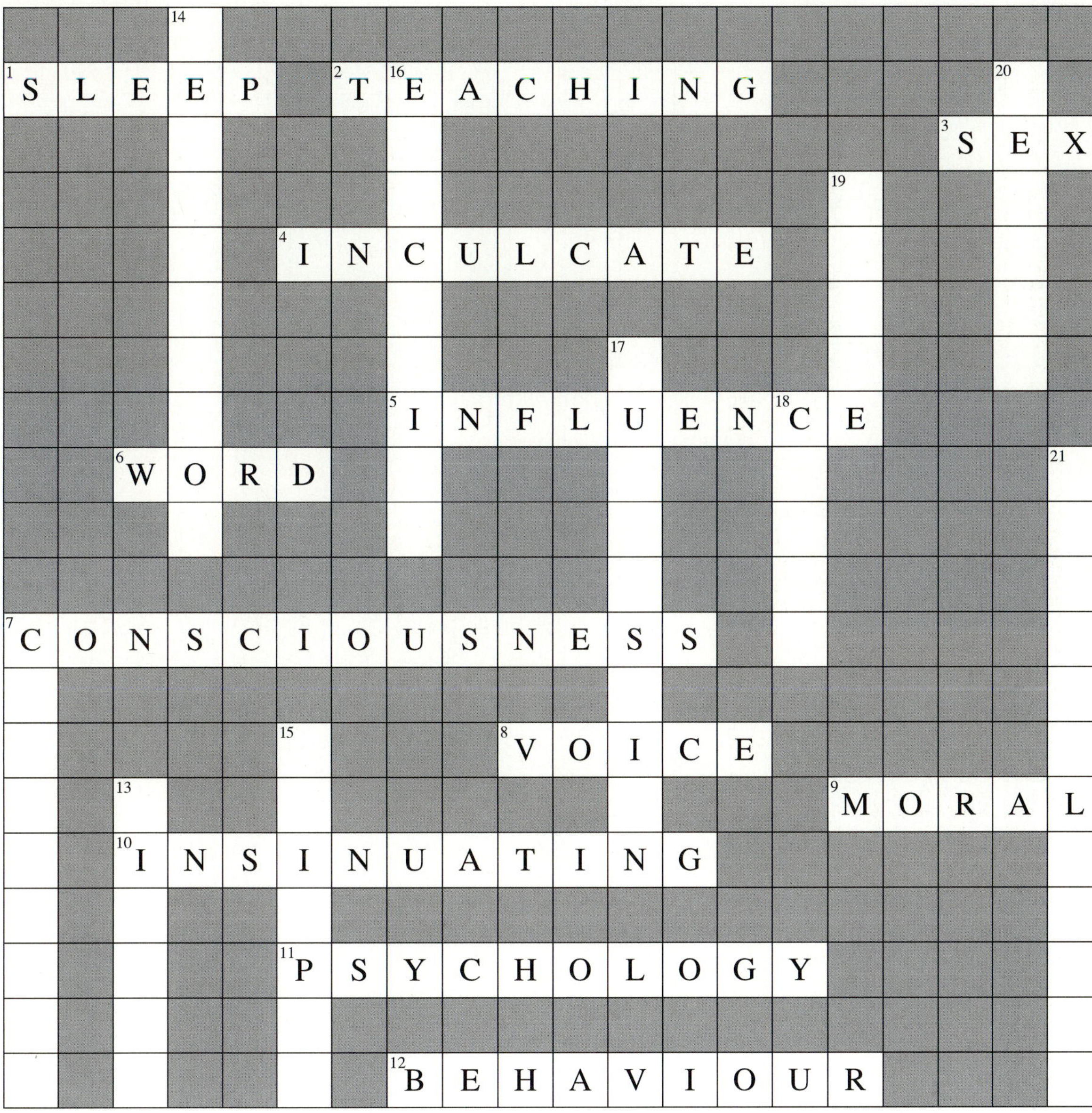

Half a crossword: “hypnopaedia” B

Work with a partner. Without using the word in question, your partner will give you an explanation for the words for numbers 1 – 12 (across) and you will write them down. You will explain your words (numbers 7 and 13 – 21, down) for your partner. Take turns.

Als Hausaufgabe sollen sich die Schülerinnen und Schüler in die Person des Direktors am Ende von Kapitel II versetzen und den nicht zu Ende gesprochenen Satz weiterführen.

Put yourself into the position of the director at the end of chapter II (p. 51, l. 27) and finish the following sentence for him.
"It therefore follows ..."

Szenenübersicht (Film)

	Opening credits	0:01:10
1	Voiceover: explanation of fertilizing process	0:01:50
2	School class in factory, praise of new society	0:03:20
3	Children's *soma*-induced sleep watched by teacher – hypno talk	0:04:40
4	Discussion of slogans and conditioning, Bernard introduced	0:06:40
5	Lenina meets someone whose invitation she refuses	0:07:00
6	Lenina discusses her private life with a friend	0:08:00
7	Lenina and Bernard decide to meet other people as well as each other	0:10:50
8	Lenina had sex with someone else	0:11:30
9	Deltas' conditioning and work	0:13:35
10	Voiceover delivering facts about the reservation and savages	0:14:15
11	Lenina and Bernard visit the reservation; their helicopter crashes	0:16:30
12	Savages approach them; there is a fight between the pilot and the attacking savages; one savage comes to their rescue	0:18:15
13	The savage, John, quotes Shakespeare and brings them to his mother, Linda, an alcoholic	0:20:00
14	John tells them about his father being an Alpha; they discuss reading books	0:22:10
15	They take John and his mother back to their world	0:23:00
16	John and his mother go for a walk in the civilized world	0:24:20
17	Delta who behaved badly is sent to 10-day reconditioning	0:25:00
18	Director meets John	0:25:50
19	Controller meets John, too; invites him to small gathering	0:26:30
20	Lenina shows Linda her apartment, asks her about John	0:27:40
21	Delta is reconditioned	0:28:30
22	John and Linda become stars at parties	0:30:25
23	Bernard talks to Controller in private. He wants to test conditioning on John	0:32:05

24	John is besieged by girls	0:33:20
25	Bernard wants to find John's father. He runs tests on him and tries to condition him	0:34:40
26	John sees Linda on *soma* holidays	0:35:15
27	John and Bernard discuss love	0:36:00
28	Interview of John and Director's comment on it	0:38:00
29	John at party – still the centre of attention, refuses Lenina	0:40:00
30	Director deletes certain files	0:40:20
31	Bernard and Lenina talk about John's refusal of her; they have sex	0:41:40
32	Delta worker is conditioned by Director to kill Bernard	0:42:50
33	John is disgusted by "party factory"	0:43:55
34	Delta worker is looking for Bernard	0:44:35
35	Bernard cannot find DNA match	0:45:30
36	John performs Shakespeare in Lenina's class	0:50:30
37	John finds his sick mother; she is taken to hospital	0:52:30
38	Lenina stays with John at hospital	0:54:40
39	Director is against John	0:55:20
40	Bernard visits Lenina; they discuss John	0:57:30
41	At home, Bernard finds out that the file was deliberately deleted	0:58:30
42	Bernard is attacked by the Delta	0:59:40
43	A Beta finds out whose file was deleted – the Director's	01:00:00
44	Director visits Linda in hospital; she dies	01:01:30
45	John sees his dead mother in hospital. He is confused about the civilized world's reaction to death	01:02:50
46	John tries to destroy *soma* and causes a riot	01:04:10
47	Discussion between Bernard, Director and Controller about John's behaviour	01:04:50
48	Beta informs Bernard about DNA match: Bernard informs the Controller about it. The Director is exposed	01:06:00
49	Bernard and John visit the Controller; John is forgiven	01:09:00
50	John tells Lenina that he is leaving. He flees to an abandoned tower, however, helicopters find him and people start hunting him	01:13:00
51	Lenina goes to John. There is some chaos; he falls off a cliff	01:14:00
52	Bernard and Lenina make love	01:15:00

53	A phone call wakes Bernard; he is appointed Director of the Hatchery	01:17:00
54	Lenina teaches her class about heroism	01:18:45
55	Lenina visits Bernard in his new office. He tells her about negative feedback from her classes. She tells him that she is pregnant	01:21:50
56	Bernard visits the Hatchery, the fitness club, his office; he seems disturbed	01:23:30
57	Bernard leaves his job and joins Lenina and their baby	01:24:40

Notizen:

Component 4:
Community, Identity, Stability

Wiederum sollte die Arbeit an *Component 4* mit der Besprechung der *Worksheets 7–9* eingeleitet werden.

In *Components 1* und *2* wurde herausgearbeitet, wie es dem Weltstaat durch Gentechnologie und „Hypnopädie" gelingt, seine Bürger seinen Zielen entsprechend zu erschaffen und zu „erziehen". In *Component 4* soll dieser Gedankengang weiter verfolgt werden, indem, ausgehend von dem Motto der *„Brave New World" „community, identity, stability"*, der Einsatz von Drogen und die Gestaltung der Freizeit als weitere Mittel der Manipulation der Menschen in themendifferenzierter Gruppenarbeit untersucht werden. Danach sollen Rolle und Arbeitsweise der Medien näher untersucht werden.

Zunächst tragen einige Schülerinnen und Schüler ihre Hausaufgabe vor, die darin bestand, die Leerstelle des Textes zu füllen, an der der Direktor am Ende von Kapitel II die Schlussfolgerung zu einem begonnenen Satz nicht mehr ausspricht. Den Schülerinnen und Schülern sollte klar geworden sein, dass der Direktor auf die Erreichung der Ziele des Weltstaates (totale Kontrolle der Bevölkerung) kommen will. So könnte der Satz z.B. folgendermaßen enden:

"It therefore follows ... *that community, identity and stability are guaranteed.*"

In einem Unterrichtsgespräch soll zunächst grob erarbeitet werden, wie es dem Weltstaat gelingt, *„social stability"* zu erreichen bzw. zu bewahren. Die folgenden Fragen sollen als Anregung dienen, um in etwa das auf der nächsten Seite abgebildete Tafelbild zu entwickeln.

We have revealed that *identity* in the World State is basically the result of genetic and behavioural engineering. Let's find out which means the World State uses to achieve *stability*. Can you name some?

- What do you think is the reason that there aren't any books (only reference books) to read in the library?
- Why does the World State say that "*History is bunk*"?
- What is the purpose of the feelies?
- Why does the World State propagate promiscuity?
- Why does the World State give out *soma*?
- Why is stability so important?
- ...

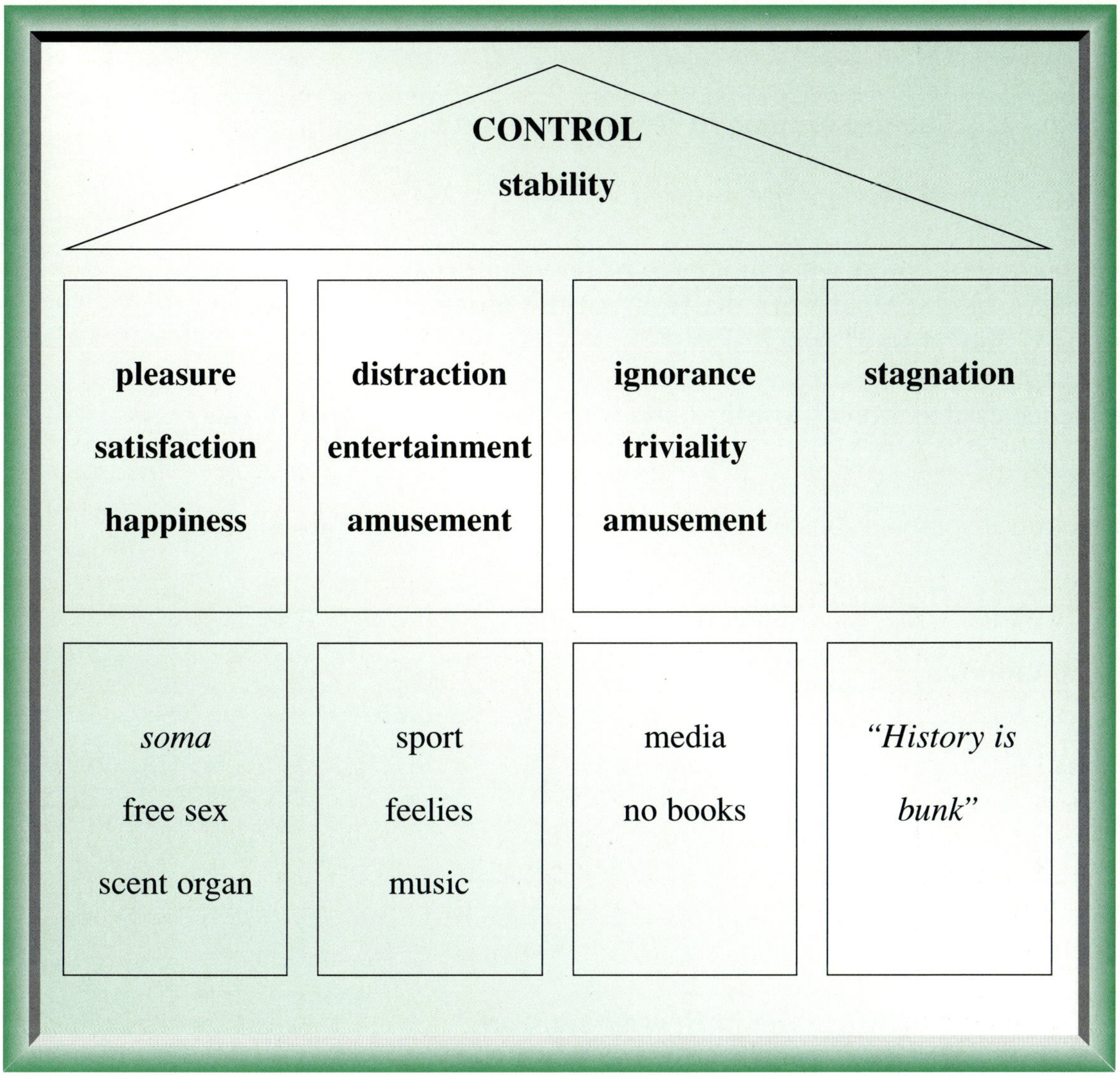

Im Anschluss sollen die angeschnittenen Themenbereiche in themendifferenzierter Gruppenarbeit weiter vertieft werden.
Die Prinzipien der Gruppenarbeit sollten gegebenenfalls vorab geklärt und z. B. auf einem Plakat an der Wand für jeden sichtbar gemacht werden.

Rules for team work:

- Everybody participates actively.
- Everybody in the team writes down the results.
- The team agrees on a "language guard" (English only!)
- The team agrees on a "time guard".
- The team agrees on a "writer" who writes down the results for the presentation.
- The team agrees on one (or several) "presenters".

Team 1: "The use of *soma* in *Brave New World*"

Assignments

1. Scan the novel and point out at what moments or on what occasions the Brave New Worlders take *soma*. Quote from the text, put the quoted passage briefly into its context and draw a short conclusion.

2. Give a one-sentence explanation as to why *soma* is necessary in the *„Brave New World"*.

3. Prepare a handout/transparency/poster ... with the most important information.

4. Present your findings to the other team.

Time available: 30 minutes

Team 2: "Cultural life in *Brave New World*"

Assignments

1. Scan the novel and make a list of the leisure-time activities the Brave New Worlders enjoy. Don't forget to give evidence from the text.

2. Find some general terms to describe the nature of these leisure activities and point out their function in the World State.

3. Prepare a handout/transparency/poster ... with the most important information.

4. Present your findings to the other team.

Time available: 30 minutes

4.1 The use of drugs

Lösungsvorschläge zu Worksheet 12

Zu erwartende Ergebnisse von *Team 1*:

Zu 1.

- Henry Foster to a glum Bernard Marx after discussing some aspects of Christianity. "What you need is a gramme of *soma."* (p. 78, ll. 17f.)
  → moment of dissatisfaction, doubts, confusion
- Lenina makes Bernard feel embarrassed in the lift when she openly tells him that she would love to go with him on a holiday. When Benito Hoover finds him in this state he suggests to take some *soma*. "What you need is a gramme of *soma*."(p. 85, ll. 8f.)
  → moment of discomfort, unease
- During their night out, Henry and Lenina go to a restaurant where *"soma* was served with the coffee". (p. 101, l. 20)
  → moment of relaxation, pleasure
- At the cabaret, Henry and Lenina take their second dose of *soma* half an hour before closing time. (cf. p. 104, ll. 10f.)
  → moment of distraction, amusement
- During the Solidarity Service at the Fordson Community Singery, dedicated *soma* tablets are used like eucharistic hosts and strawberry ice-cream *soma* can be compared to the wine during a Christian mass. (cf. p. 108, ll. 4ff.)
  → moment of solidarity, community, annihilation
- When Bernard feels gloomy one afternoon, Lenina advises him to take a half-gramme raspberry sundae at the ice-cream *soma* bar. "Remember, one cubic centimeter cures ten gloomy sentiments." (p. 117, ll. 14f.)
  → moment of melancholy, misery
- When Bernard tries to make Lenina understand that he would rather be free from conditioning she reacts by saying: "Why don't you take *soma* when you have these dreadful ideas of yours. You'd forget all about them. And instead of feeling miserable you'd be jolly." (p. 119, l. 29 – p. 120, l. 2).
  → moment of misery, doubts, thinking
- When Bernard is furious about the director's decision to send him into exile on an island, he agrees to swallow four tablets of *soma.* (cf. p. 143, ll. 22f.)
  → moment of rage
- At the reservation, Lenina is shocked by the sight of an old man and wants to take some *soma,* but she has left the bottle at the rest-house. So "Lenina was left to face the horrors of Malpais unaided." (p. 142, l. 11)
  → moment of horror, confusion, shock
- When Lenina cannot stand what she witnesses during a violent fertility ritual on the reservation, she thinks that *soma* would help her. "Too awful! All that blood! ... Oh, I wish I had my *soma.*" (p. 147, ll. 24f.)
  → moment of shock
- At the end of the day on the reservation "Lenina felt herself entitled, after a day of queerness and horror, to a complete and absolute holiday. As soon as they got back to the rest-house, she swallowed six half-gramme tablets of *soma.* […]" (p. 174, ll. 20ff.)
  → moment of stress

- The factory workers get a ration of *soma* when they have finished their work. "They get it after their work is over. Four half-gramme tablets. Six on Saturdays." (p. 202, ll. 5f., cf. also p. 251, l. 12)
  → moment of reward
- When Lenina feels disappointed because John does not want to spend the night with her, she eases her pain with *soma*. "One gramme, she decided, would not be enough; hers had been more than a one-gramme affliction." (p. 210, ll. 11f.)
  → moment of pain, distress, affliction
- When Bernard realizes that there is a kind of mutual understanding between John and Helmholtz, he resorts to *soma* because he does not want to feel jealous. "He was ashamed of his jealousy and alternately made efforts of will and took *soma* to keep himself from feeling it." (p. 222, ll. 5ff.)
  → moment of jealousy, distress, confusion
- Fanny advises her friend Lenina to take *soma* to forget John because he does not seem to want to return her love. (cf. p. 228, l. 15)
  → moment of misery, distress, "lovesickness"
- The policemen try to calm down the upset masses of workers with *soma* vapour. (cf. p. 258, ll. 3f.)
  → moment of unrest
- When Bernard suffers a nervous breakdown because of Mustapha Mond's decision to send him into exile, Mustapha Mond orders: "Bring three men and take Mr Marx into a bedroom. Give him a good *soma* vaporization and then put him to bed and leave him." (p. 271, ll. 5ff.)
  → moment of stress, agitation

Zu 2.
Since the World State wants to achieve the total control of its citizens, it has to avoid or take care of moments of emotional instability and that is why *soma* is necessary to calm people and make them happy by enabling them to escape from reality.

Während Team 1 seine Ergebnisse präsentiert, macht Team 2 sich Notizen zu Inhalt, Sprache und Präsentation. Anschließend werden die inhaltlichen Aspekte gegebenenfalls erläutert und ergänzt, die sprachlichen Vorzüge und Fehler kommentiert sowie die Art der Präsentation evaluiert.
Ausgehend von den Ergebnissen von Team 1 sollen in einem folgenden Unterrichtsgespräch durch einen Vergleich zum Drogenkonsum in unserer Gesellschaft die Parallelen und Unterschiede herausgestellt werden. Höchstwahrscheinlich werden die Schülerinnen und Schüler zuerst den Konsum von Alkohol und Drogen im engeren Sinne (Marihuana, Kokain, etc.) und die Einnahme von Beruhigungsmitteln und Amphetaminen nennen. Da heutzutage in vielen Klassen auch Kinder sitzen, die unter den Krankheiten ADS (Aufmerksamkeits-Defizit-Syndrom) und ADHS (Aufmerksamkeits-Defizit-Hyperaktivitäts-Störung) leiden und medizinisch behandelt werden, ist damit zu rechnen, dass auch die Verabreichung von entsprechenden beruhigenden Medikamenten (die bekanntesten sind *Ritalin* und *Prozak)* bekannt ist.

Mögliche Impulse:

- Can you see any parallels to our society?
- Why do people take drugs or consume alcohol?

- What do people do to forget about their problems?
- Name the effects and consequences of the consumption of drugs.
- What can you do to calm a very upset person?
- ...

Die Ergebnisse könnten folgendermaßen an der Tafel festgehalten werden:

	soma	**alcohol, drugs**	**behavioural drugs**
occasion:	emotional stress	emotional stress	ADD (Attention Deficit Disorder) or ADHD (Attention Deficit Hyper-activity Disorder)
function:	escape	escape	calm kids, make them fit for school
effect:	happiness no negative effects	physical problems hangover addiction social problems	only superficial treatment
	→ happiness, encouraged by the World State → manipulation, loss of self-determina-tion	no solution	no solution

Als Hausaufgabe bietet es sich an, die Gesprächsergebnisse, die stichwortartig an der Tafel stehen, in einem zusammenhängenden Text zu verschriftlichen.

Compare the role of *soma* in *Brave New World* to the role of drugs in our society.

4.2 Cultural life

Die nächste Stunde beginnt mit dem Vortragen der Hausaufgabe, wodurch die Rolle von *soma* als Manipulationsmittel des Weltstaates wieder in Erinnerung gerufen wird. Dann präsentiert Team 2 seine Arbeitsergebnisse, während Team 1 aufgefordert wird, sich Notizen zu Inhalt, Sprache und Präsentation zu machen. Anschließend werden die inhaltlichen Aspekte gegebenenfalls erläutert und ergänzt, die Sprache kommentiert und die Präsentationsweise von Team 2 evaluiert.

Lösungsvorschläge zu Worksheet 12

Zu erwartende Ergebnisse von *Team 2:*

Zu 1.

leisure-time activities in *Brave New World*

- Centrifugal Bumble-Puppy (p. 52)
- Musical Bridge (p. 64)
- Going out (p. 64)
- Obstacle golf (pp. 84, 88, 97 etc.)
- Riemann-surface tennis (p. 87)
- (Westminster Abbey) Cabaret (p. 101)
- Enjoying the Scent and Colour Organ (p. 102)
- Listening to synthetic music (p. 102, p. 112 etc.)
- Dancing (p. 103, p. 112)
- Travelling (p. 82, p. 94 etc.)
- Watching sports (p. 117)
- Solidarity Service (p. 105)
- Community Singing (p. 105)
- Electromagnetic golf (p. 107, p. 116)
- Dining (p. 101)
- Swimming (p. 116)
- Escalator-squash (p. 129)
- Feelies (p. 200, pp. 205f.)
- TV (p. 129 etc.)
- Sex (p. 234 etc.)
- *Soma* holidays

Zu 2.

The *Brave New World* leisure-time activities are all practised in groups and aimed at the distraction and entertainment of the people. They ensure that the people are never alone and constantly happy with superficial, mindless amusements. The function of these kinds of activities is to prevent the Brave New Worlders from questioning the State and endangering its stability. The World State offers these activities in order to be in control, to manipulate its citizens.

Im Anschluss soll nun die Freizeitgestaltung in *Brave New World* mit der in unserer Gesellschaft verglichen werden. Dies soll wieder in einem Unterrichtsgespräch erfolgen, dessen Ergebnisse stichwortartig an der Tafel festgehalten werden. Es wird sich ergeben, dass die meisten Menschen heute ähnliche Freizeitaktivitäten verfolgen wie die Menschen in Huxleys Roman. Sie suchen oberflächliche Unterhaltung und Zerstreuung, was die Gefahr der Passivität und des Kontrollverlustes birgt.

Mögliche Impulse:

- What do you do in your free time?
- Identify the aim of leisure activities.
- ...

leisure-time activities in our society

- sports
- computer games
- TV
- hanging out with friends
- movies
- shopping
- (reading)
- …

→ entertainment, distraction → superficial, mindless

danger: passivity, loss of control, loss of autonomy

Zur Vertiefung des Themas erhalten die Schülerinnen und Schüler die Hausaufgabe, ein Zitat des Soziologen Neil Postman zu kommentieren.

Comment on the following statement by Neil Postman: "Today we must look at the city of Las Vegas, Nevada, as a metaphor of our national character and aspiration, its symbol a thirty-foot-high cardboard picture of a slot machine and a chorus girl."
(Neil Postman: *Amusing Ourselves to Death*. New York: Penguin Books 1985, p. 3)

4.3 The role of the media

Die nächste Stunde beginnt mit dem Vortragen der Hausaufgabe, die einerseits an das Thema der vergangenen Stunde (unser auf Zerstreuung und Vergnügen ausgerichtetes Freizeitverhalten) anknüpft, andererseits auch als Einstieg in das Thema dieser Stunde dient. Im Folgenden sollen einige Aspekte der Medien in *Brave New World* analysiert und ein Vergleich mit der Aktionsweise der Medien in unserer heutigen Gesellschaft angestrebt werden.
In diesem Zusammenhang bieten sich zwei Filme als mögliche Referatsthemen an, die sich mit der Rolle der Medien beschäftigen: *The Truman Show* (Peter Weir, 1998) und *Pleasantville* (Gary Ross, 1998). Beide Filme sind Mediensatiren und könnten unter Berücksichtigung der Punkte der *Kopiervorlage S. 40 (Component 2)* von Schülerinnen und Schülern selbstständig analysiert und präsentiert werden.
Um sich einen Überblick über die Medienlandschaft in *Brave New World* zu verschaffen, werden die Schülerinnen und Schüler aufgefordert, die entsprechende Textstelle zu lesen und die einzelnen Abteilungen der Medien des Weltstaates aufzulisten.
In einem anschließenden Unterrichtsgespräch wird deren Funktion geklärt, die darin besteht, die Menschen zu unterhalten und von kritischem Denken abzulenken. Die einzelnen Medien wenden sich zielgruppengerecht an die einzelnen Gesellschaftsschichten der *Brave New World* und dienen dem Weltstaat somit auch als Manipulations- und Kontrollinstrument, das für *stability* sorgt. Der Name des Wolkenkratzers, in dem die Medien untergebracht sind *(Propaganda House)*, ein „*telling name*", spricht deutlich für sich und so können die Definitionen einsprachiger Wörterbücher leicht zur Klärung der Aufgabe der Medien beitragen.

Ein(e) Schüler(in) (oder die Lehrperson) hält die Ergebnisse auf Folie oder an der Tafel fest.

Make a list of the different departments of the media in the World State as they are presented on p. 91, l. 14 – p. 92, l. 4.

Explain the name of the building, "Propaganda House", (p. 92, l. 3) with the help of a monolingual dictionary and point out the function the media are meant to fulfil in *Brave New World*.

Propaganda House

College of Emotional Engineering

Research laboratories
Sound-track writers
Synthetic composers

Television
Feeling Picture

Synthetic Voice and Music

<u>Newspapers</u>
The Hourly Radio (upper caste)
The Gamma Gazette
The Delta-Mirror ("one-syllable words only")

The function of the media is to entertain, to distract. They are designed to meet the needs of the people according to their social conditioning.

→ propaganda
→ manipulation
→ stability
→ control

Propaganda: ideas or statements that may be false or exaggerated and that are used in order to gain support for a political leader, party, etc. (*Oxford Advanced Learner's Dictionary*)
Propaganda: is information, often exaggerated or false information which an organization publishes or broadcasts in order to influence people. (*Cobuild English Learner's Dictionary*)
Propaganda: information which is false or which emphasizes just one part of a situation, used by a government or political group to make people agree with them. (*Longman Dictionary of Contemporary English*)

Die Hausaufgabe zur nächsten Stunde besteht darin, Kapitel XVIII erneut zu lesen und eine Zusammenfassung zu verfassen sowie kurze Informationen zu Darwin und Bonaparte zu ermitteln.

Give a summary of chapter XVIII and gather some basic information about Charles Darwin and Bonaparte.

Zur Vergegenwärtigung des Inhalts wird zu Beginn der folgenden Stunde die Zusammenfassung von Kapitel XVIII vorgetragen. Dies könnte in Form eines *snowball-summary* erfolgen. Ein Schüler beginnt mit dem ersten Satz, ein anderer Schüler/eine Schülerin schließt den nächsten Satz an usw. Folgende Punkte sollten erwähnt werden:

Summary of chapter XVIII

John feels disgusted by the *Brave New World* society and seeks peace and quiet in a lonely area on England's South coast in an abandoned lighthouse. He feels guilty because of Linda's death and his longing for Lenina. That is why he tries to purify himself by whipping himself as punishment for his sins. When reporters find out about this penitential rite, they film him secretly and broadcast every move he makes. In this way he becomes a tourist attraction. When John recognizes Lenina among the curious masses, he gets into a wild rage, blindly attacks her and starts a mass orgy. When he wakes up the next morning and realizes what he has done, he hangs himself.

Dann werden die Schülerinnen und Schüler aufgefordert, in Partnerarbeit die Mittel aufzudecken, mit denen Huxley seine Missbilligung der Arbeitsweise der Journalisten zum Ausdruck bringt. Hier kommen auch die in der Hausaufgabe gesammelten Informationen zu Darwin und Bonaparte zur Anwendung.

Explain how Huxley expresses his disapproval of the reporters' practices in chapter XVIII.

Die Schülerinnen und Schüler werden in etwa zu den folgenden Ergebnissen kommen, die auf Folie oder an der Tafel festgehalten werden:

The description of the reporters

- *like turkey buzzards settling on a corpse (p. 295, ll. 7f.)*
- *startled as though by the bite of a snake (p. 295, l. 20)*
- *the vermin evidently became bored (p. 299, l. 4)*
- *the arrival overhead of a great swarm of helicopters (p. 302, ll. 4f.)*
- *like locusts they came (p. 303, l. 6)*
- *and from out of the bellies of these giant grasshoppers (p. 303, ll. 9f.)*
- *like swine about the trough (p. 307, l. 4)*

Huxley uses a lot of images (metaphors, similes) from the animal kingdom to describe the reporters and their practices. The animals he chooses to compare are usually considered as very unpleasant and their behaviour as brutal and disgusting.

By giving the reporter the name *Darwin Bonaparte* (p. 300, l. 15), Huxley insinuates that the reporter acts ruthlessly according to Charles Darwin's idea of the "survival of the fittest". The name *Bonaparte is* associated with military strategies, invading somebody's territory and an arrogant attitude.

In einer folgenden kurzen Gruppenarbeitsphase soll die Arbeitsweise der Journalisten mit möglichst vielen Adjektiven beschrieben werden, die in Form eines *clusters* auf Folie präsentiert werden. Dabei sollten Wörterbücher zur Verfügung stehen. Wenn die Schülerinnen und Schüler in der Hausaufgabe die Arbeitsweise der Medien in *Brave New World* mit denen der Massenmedien in unserer heutigen Gesellschaft vergleichen, werden sie zu dem Schluss kommen, dass unsere Massenmedien sich genau dieser Praktiken bedienen.

Work in groups of four and make a cluster of adjectives that describe the practices of the media in *Brave New World*.

Compare the practices of the mass media in our contemporary society to those of Huxley's *Brave New World*.

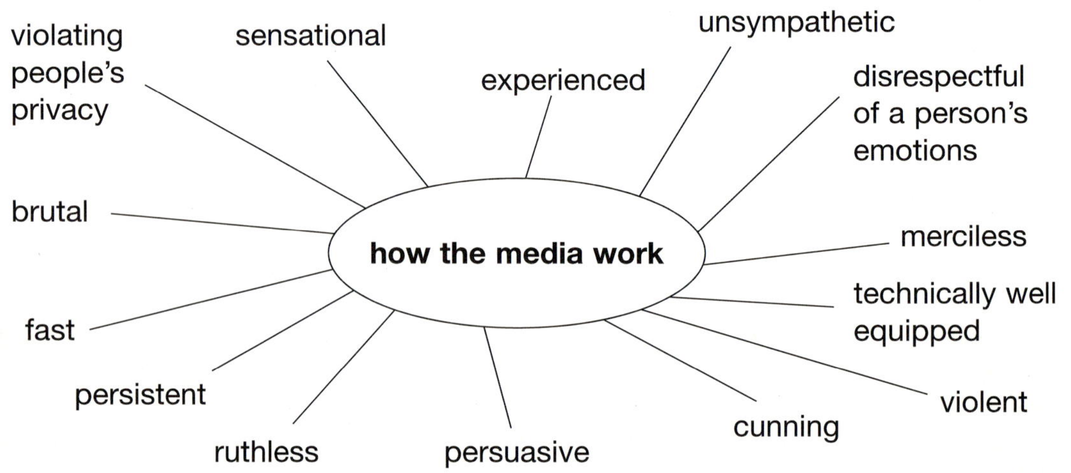

Anschließend soll untersucht werden, mit welchen Mitteln die Regisseure des Films dem Zuschauer die skrupellose Aufdringlichkeit der Reporter näher bringen. Dazu werden die Szenen 50 und 51 mit folgendem *while-viewing assignment* (mehrmals) präsentiert.

Watch scenes 50 and 51 closely and make a list of the means the directors use to make the viewer feel the brutal practices of the media.

Es ist zu erwarten, dass folgende Punkte genannt werden:

Devices the directors of the film use to show the brutal practices of the media in scenes 50 and 51.

Scene 50:

- interrupted voice-over commentaries of different TV stations
- jump cuts
- fast cuts between John and the reporters
- sudden silence, close-up of John, beautiful sunset as background → cut → contrast: heavy night-time traffic in London
- interrupted voice-overs of different TV and radio stations
- cut: day-time, silence, close-up of John in beautiful landscape
- sudden descending of loud helicopters
- high angle on John
- reporters are running, using microphones with long sticks
- cut: London: people on their way home stare at John who is exposed on TV screens like an animal in the zoo

Scene 51:

- at night the reporters' strong searchlights are hunting John
- the reporters are running, shouting
- hectic searchlights looking for their victim
- the blinding light of an approaching helicopter makes John fall off a cliff
- the helicopter light focuses on the dead John
- sight of laughing, cheering reporters happy with the sensation

Notizen:

Component 5:
Wrapping up the Novel

Im Folgenden werden die unterschiedlichsten Aufgabentypen angeboten, die man zu einem Lernzirkel zusammenfassen kann. Der Vorteil bei der Arbeit mit Stationen liegt darin, dass alle Schülerinnen und Schüler ständig aktiv sind und selber feststellen können, ob sie sich an alle wichtigen Aspekte des Romans erinnern und mit ihnen arbeiten können (Lernerautonomie).

Die Materialien werden auf *Worksheets* präsentiert; eine kurze tabellarische Übersicht gibt der Lehrperson die Möglichkeit, auszuwählen, welche Stationen sie anbieten möchte. Es gibt sowohl Stationen, die von den Schülerinnen und Schülern völlig selbstständig bearbeitet und kontrolliert werden können, als auch Stationen, deren Ergebnisse im Kurs präsentiert werden, sowie Stationen, an denen die Schülerinnen und Schüler sich in Form von Partnerarbeit gegenseitig kontrollieren sollten. Man könnte als Vorgabe dem Kurs mitteilen, dass fünf Stationen obligatorisch sind, von denen eine eine Präsentationsphase erfordert. Die Schülerinnen und Schüler könnten dann selber darauf achten, dass sie nicht dieselbe Station mehrfach präsentieren. Diese Absprachen sollten auf Englisch und ohne Mitwirkung der Lehrperson erfolgen. Die Lösungsblätter werden als Kopie zu den entsprechenden Stationen gegeben, sodass die Lösungen dem Kurs zur Verfügung gestellt werden und die Schülerinnen und Schüler leicht selbst kontrollieren können, wie viele Teilaufgaben sie richtig gelöst haben.

Diese Arbeitsform erfreut sich bei den Schülerinnen und Schülern in der Regel großer Akzeptanz; sie fühlen sich ernst genommen und missbrauchen nicht die Tatsache, dass sie sich selbst kontrollieren dürfen, zum Schummeln. Ein Laufzettel erleichtert den Kursteilnehmern die Orientierung über die bereits abgeleisteten Stationen. Je nach Anzahl der gewählten Stationen wird die Arbeit selbst bis zu einer Doppelstunde dauern, die Präsentationsphase wird ebenfalls eine bis zwei Unterrichtsstunden in Anspruch nehmen.

In der Tabelle kann man zusammengefasst sehen, welche Aufgabentypen welche Fähigkeiten der Schülerinnen und Schüler aktivieren sollen und welche Medien man für die entsprechende Station braucht. Das *Worksheet* zu Station 2 bezieht sich auf den Anfang der Seite 3 (Kassette 2) der Ausgabe des Hörbuchs von *Harper Collins Audio Books,* den Beginn von *Chapter X*. Wenn man das Hörbuch nicht besitzt, kann man ebenso gut die Kassette selbst besprechen.

Die unter der Tabelle aufgeführten Arbeitsanweisungen können einmal kopiert und an der Station in einer Prospekthülle hinterlegt werden. Die benötigten Kopien werden ebenfalls in einer Prospekthülle ausgelegt. Die Lösungen werden in einfacher Kopie in einem Pappdeckel mit deutlicher Aufschrift „Solution“ hinterlegt. Die Schülerinnen und Schüler benötigen lediglich Stifte und Papier.

	Aufgabentyp	Fähigkeit	Medien/Material
1	Multiple Choice Test, Wordsearch	Lesen, Sprechen	Kopien, Novel
2	Hörverstehen (Romantext)	Hören, Schreiben	drei bis vier Walkmen, Kopien
3	Collage erstellen	Lesen, Informationen suchen	Internetzugang, Zeitschriften, A3-Pappen
4	Kreatives Schreiben, Reiseführer *Brave New World* schreiben	Schreiben	Novel
5	Filmausschnitt mit Roman vergleichen	Verstehen, Schreiben, Lesen	TV/Video, Novel, Kopien
6	Rollenspiel	Schreiben, Sprechen	Novel
7	Hörverstehen (Song)	Lesen, Hören, Sprechen	Discman, Kopien

Station 1 *(Worksheet 13a)*, 1:
1. Copy the correct conclusion of the 14 sentences onto the worksheet.
2. You may use the copy of the novel that you find here.
3. When finished, compare your results with the solutions given on the solution sheet.

Station 1 *(Worksheet 13b)*, 2:
1. Find 12 words in the grid that have to do with *Brave New World.*
2. When finished, compare your findings with the solutions given on the solution sheet.
3. Work with a partner. Choose one of the words that you have found and explain its meaning in the context of the novel. Take turns.

Station 2 *(Worksheet 14)*:
1. Listen to the text on the cassette.
2. Read the text on the worksheet.
3. Listen again to the text and fill in the missing words.
4. When finished, compare your results with the solutions given on the solution sheet.

Station 3:
1. Discuss what you think is most important about the novel *Brave New World.*
2. Browse through the magazines and decide if there are any pictures you want to use for producing a poster about *Brave New World* that illustrates your ideas.
3. Use the Internet for research on your idea of what *Brave New World* is about.
4. Create a poster that you can present to your classmates.

Station 4:
Imagine that we could visit the "*Brave New World*" as tourists. Write a chapter for a travel guide that focuses on cultural differences and that would enable us to understand the behaviour of the Brave New Worlders so that we can behave correctly.
Add some brief hints on interesting places to see and things to do.

Station 5:
1. Read pages 306 – 308.
2. Describe in your own words how the novel *Brave New World* ends.
3. Imagine you are a Hollywood director and you want to make a film of *Brave New World.* Describe briefly how you would film the end of the story. Would you make changes? What would happen to John in your film?
4. Watch scenes 50 and 51 (01:13:00 – 01:15:00). What do you like about the way the film shows John? What don't you like?
5. Compare your version of a possible ending for the book with the film.
6. There are about 10 more minutes of film left. Can you think of what might happen during that time?
7. Prepare a short presentation of your work for your classmates.

Station 6:
The government of *Brave New World* has been toppled by a group of inhabitants from the reservations who want to take their revenge for having been mistreated by the so-called civilized world. Mustapha Mond is arrested and put to trial.
1. Decide who wants to play whose role. You need Mustapha Mond, a prosecutor and a judge. If your group has more than three members you might want to introduce a witness or a lawyer who helps Mustapha Mond with his defence.
2. Take notes and play a scene in court when Mr Mond is defending himself against the prosecutor's accusations. Take into consideration what you have read about the government's motives for introducing *soma* and hypnopaedia and forbidding literature.
3. Practice your role-play and be ready to present your scene to your classmates.

Station 7 *(Worksheet 15)*:
1. Skim the lyrics of the song *Brave New World* by Iron Maiden.
2. Listen to the CD and put the passages into their correct order by numbering them.
3. Listen again and check your answers.
4. When finished compare your results with the lyrics given on the solution sheet.
5. Work with a partner. Choose a line or a stanza and comment on it.

Station 1

Multiple Choice Test:

1. What is the name of the process that allows the Hatchery to produce many clones from a single egg?
   - ☐ the Podansky Process
   - ☐ the Trotsky Process
   - ☐ the Bokanovsky Process
   - ☐ Centrifugal Bumble-puppy

2. Deltas are not supposed to like flowers because
   - ☐ flowers are grown for Alphas only.
   - ☐ loving nature does not make them consume anything.
   - ☐ flowers are regarded as poisonous.
   - ☐ Deltas are not allowed to leave their factories.

3. Bernard Marx is wretched because Lenina
   - ☐ behaves like a regular English girl and goes out with everybody.
   - ☐ does not want to go out with him.
   - ☐ refuses to go out with the Savage.
   - ☐ loves Benito Hoover.

4. Bernard Marx attends a Community Sing and experiences
   - ☐ a wonderful feeling of community with his group.
   - ☐ a close relationship to Fifi Bradlaugh.
   - ☐ no rapture and bliss.
   - ☐ a real orgy.

5. The Director was in New Mexico 25 years ago and
   - ☐ now is strictly against Bernard's going there.
   - ☐ tells Bernard about the horrible incident that happened there.
   - ☐ thinks it was the best trip of his life.
   - ☐ still goes there regularly for holidays.

6. Lenina's reaction to her first encounter with the Indians is
   - ☐ happiness.
   - ☐ indifference.
   - ☐ fear.
   - ☐ disgust.

7. Linda lives in
   - ☐ a very clean hamlet.
   - ☐ a very dirty, small hut.
   - ☐ a big house with other families.
   - ☐ a special house in the middle of the village.

8. John has learned most of his English and his phrases from
   - ☐ the Bible.
   - ☐ John Milton's works.
   - ☐ Linda and her boyfriends.
   - ☐ William Shakespeare's works.

9. When Linda meets the Director in London, he
   - ☐ turns pale and appears to be very humiliated.
   - ☐ is overwhelmed by happiness.
   - ☐ gives a party in her honour.
   - ☐ hides from her.

10. When Bernard Marx introduces the Savage to London society
    - ☐ he is laughed at.
    - ☐ he is arrested.
    - ☐ Helmholtz refuses to be his friend any longer.
    - ☐ he feels wonderful because he is suddenly accepted.

11. Helmholtz breaks out in uncontrollable laughter when listening to John's reading of Romeo and Juliet because
    - ☐ he mistakes the tragedy for a comedy.
    - ☐ due to his conditioning he cannot understand the feelings presented in that play.
    - ☐ he thinks John does not speak English at all.
    - ☐ he is reminded of hypnopaedia.

12. When John visits the dying Linda in hospital
    - ☐ all the nurses are very sympathetic.
    - ☐ there is a preacher.
    - ☐ there is a group of children totally bewildered by the sight of a dying older woman.
    - ☐ Linda recovers from her illness.

13. The Controller decides to punish Bernard Marx.
    - ☐ He sentences him to 20 years in prison.
    - ☐ He has him killed instantaneously.
    - ☐ He takes away his job and orders him to work in a factory.
    - ☐ He sends him into exile on an island.

14. The Savage flees from civilization
    - ☐ and goes back to his reservation.
    - ☐ and is hunted down by journalists.
    - ☐ and takes Lenina with him to an island.
    - ☐ and lives as a hermit in the woods.

Now think of three similar questions of your own and write them down for your classmates. Don't forget to give a solution on an extra sheet.

Solutions (Worksheet 13a)

1. the Bokanovsky Process
2. loving nature does not make them consume anything.
3. behaves like a regular English girl and goes out with everybody.
4. no rapture and bliss.
5. tells Bernard about the horrible incident that happened there.
6. disgust.
7. a very dirty, small hut.
8. William Shakespeare's works.
9. turns pale and appears to be very humiliated.
10. he feels wonderful because he is suddenly accepted.
11. due to his conditioning he cannot understand the feelings presented in that play.
12. there is a group of children totally bewildered by the sight of a dying older woman.
13. He sends him into exile on an island.
14. and is hunted down by journalists.

Station 1

1. **Find 12 words in the following grid that have to do with *Brave New World.* You can read them in 8 different ways: ↑↓ ⇄ ⤢ ⤡**

***Brave New World*: Wordsearch**

Y	E	G	X	K	P	G	J	P	I	N	R	W	S	N
H	L	N	E	I	A	A	O	O	A	A	X	Y	T	A
T	N	E	M	N	I	A	T	R	E	T	N	E	A	M
A	Y	R	E	S	U	I	A	H	C	C	Q	G	B	M
X	T	F	E	F	I	M	O	L	X	G	P	A	I	A
I	I	A	U	S	O	R	O	L	S	K	I	C	L	G
P	U	J	I	S	E	N	U	A	Y	D	B	L	I	K
R	C	K	Y	Q	I	R	D	O	E	U	S	U	T	R
N	S	Z	W	N	V	B	V	A	I	H	H	Y	Y	X
I	I	R	G	S	I	K	P	A	V	V	D	L	B	D
V	M	U	T	W	K	O	Y	B	T	D	A	F	D	Z
U	O	D	V	N	N	S	D	T	K	I	K	H	I	S
I	R	Q	X	P	E	G	A	V	A	S	O	K	E	E
N	P	B	Y	Q	Q	V	D	Q	C	K	D	N	U	B
M	Z	H	C	O	N	S	U	M	E	R	I	S	M	J

2. **Work with a partner. Choose one of the words you have found and explain its meaning in the context of the novel. Take turns.**

Solutions (Worksheet 13b)

Y	+	+	+	+	+	+	+	+	+	+	+	+	S	+
+	L	+	+	+	+	+	+	+	+	+	+	+	T	A
T	N	E	M	N	I	A	T	R	E	T	N	E	A	M
+	Y	R	E	S	+	+	A	+	C	+	+	+	B	M
+	T	+	E	F	I	M	+	L	+	+	+	A	I	A
+	I	+	+	S	O	R	O	+	+	+	I	+	L	G
+	U	+	+	S	E	N	U	+	+	D	+	+	I	+
+	C	+	+	+	I	R	+	O	E	+	+	+	T	+
+	S	+	+	N	+	+	V	A	I	+	+	+	Y	+
+	I	+	G	+	+	+	P	A	+	V	+	+	+	+
+	M	+	+	+	+	O	+	+	T	+	A	+	+	+
+	O	+	+	+	N	+	+	+	+	I	+	H	+	+
+	R	+	+	P	E	G	A	V	A	S	O	+	E	+
+	P	+	Y	+	+	+	+	+	+	+	+	N	+	B
+	+	H	C	O	N	S	U	M	E	R	I	S	M	+

(Over, Down, Direction)
BEHAVIOURISM (15,14, NW)
CLONING (10, 4, SW)
CONSUMERISM (4, 15, E)
ENTERTAINMENT (13, 3, W)
FEELY (5, 5, NW)
GAMMA (15, 6, N)
HYPNOPAEDIA (3, 15, NE)
PROMISCUITY (2, 14, N)
RESERVATION (3, 4, SE)
SAVAGE (11, 13, W)
SOMA (5, 7, NE)
STABILITY (14, 1, S)

Station 2

The hands of all the four thousand electric clocks in all the Bloomsbury Centre's four thousand rooms marked twenty-seven minutes past two.
"This hive of industry," as the Director was fond of calling it, was in the full buzz of work. Everyone was busy, everything in ordered motion. [...]
The dynamos purred in the sub-basement, the lifts rushed up and down. [...]
_________________ (1) ! the hive was humming, busily, joyfully. Blithe was the singing of the young girls over their test tubes, the predestinators whistled as they worked, and in the Decanting Room what glorious jokes were cracked above the empty bottles! But the Director's face as he entered the Fertilizing Room with Henry Foster, was grave, wooden with severity.
"A public example," he was saying. "In this room, because it _________________ (2) more high-caste workers than any other in this Centre. I have told him to meet me here at half-past two."
"He does his work very well," put in Henry with hypocritical generosity.
"I know. But that's all the more reason for severity. His intellectual eminence carries with it corresponding moral ___________________________ (3).
The greater a man's talents, the greater his power to lead astray. It is better that one should suffer than that many should be corrupted. [...] No offence is so heinous as _________________ (4) of behaviour. Murder kills only the individual – and, after all, what is an individual? [...] We can make a new one with the greatest ease – as many as we like. Unorthodoxy threatens more than the life of a mere individual; it strikes at society itself. Ah, but here he comes."
Bernard had entered the room and was advancing between the rows of fertilizers towards them. A veneer of jaunty ___________________________ (5) thinly concealed his nervousness. [...]
"Good morning, Director. You asked me to come and speak to you here." [...]
"Yes, Mr Marx," said the Director portentously. "I did ask you to come to me here. You returned from your holiday last night, I understand." [...]
Then, suddenly _________________ (6) his voice, "Ladies and gentlemen," he trumpeted, "ladies and gentlemen."
The singing of the girls over their test-tubes, the preoccupied whistling of the Microscopists, suddenly ceased. There was a profound silence; every one looked round.
"Ladies and gentlemen," the Director repeated once more, "excuse me for _________________ (7) your labours. A painful duty constrains me. The security and stability of Society are in danger. Yes, in danger, ladies and gentlemen. This man," he pointed accusingly at Bernard, "this man who stands before you here, this Alpha-Plus to whom so much has been given, and from whom, in _________________ (8), so much must be expected, this colleague of yours – or should I anticipate and say this ex-colleague? – has grossly betrayed the trust imposed in him. By his heretical views on sport and *soma,* by the scandalous unorthodoxy of his sex-life, by his refusal to obey the teachings of _________________ (9) and behave out of office hours 'like a babe in a bottle'" (here the Director made the sign of the T), "he has proved himself an enemy of Society, a subverter, ladies and gentlemen, of all Order and Stability, a conspirator against Civilization itself. For this reason I propose to dismiss him, to dismiss him with _________________ (10) from the post he has held in this Centre; I

propose forthwith to apply for his transference to a Sub-Centre of the lowest order and, that his punishment may serve the best interest of Society, as far as possible removed from any important Centre of population. In ________________ (11) he will have small opportunity to lead others astray by his unfordly example." The Director paused: then, folding his arms, he turned impressively to Bernard. "Marx," he said, "can you show any reason why I should not now execute the judgment passed upon you?"
"Yes, I can," Bernard answered. [...] "Certainly. But it's in the passage. One moment." Bernard hurried to the door and threw it open. "Come in," he commanded, and the ________________ (12) came in and showed itself.

Additional question:
Who comes in? ____________________ (13)

Aldous Huxley, *Brave New World*, pp. 180–185; © 1992 Philipp Reclam jun. GmbH & Co., Stuttgart; Copyright © 1932, 1946 by Aldous Huxley

Solutions (Worksheet 14)

1. Buzz, buzz
2. contains
3. responsibilities
4. unorthodoxy
5. self-confidence
6. raising
7. interrupting
8. consequence
9. Our Ford
10. ignominy
11. Iceland
12. reason
13. Linda

Station 7

Brave New World

A brave new world in a brave new world A brave new world in a brave new world
Wilderness house of pain Makes no sense of it all
Your are planned and you are damned In this brave new world
Lost my love, lost my life In this garden of fear
All is lost sold your soul To this brave new world
Dragon Kings Dying Queens Where is salvation now Lost my life lost my dreams
I have seen many things In a lifetime alone
A brave new world in a brave new world A brave new world in a brave new world
Dying Swans twisted wings Beauty not needed here
Rip the bones from my flesh Silent screams laughing here
Mother love is no more Bring the savage back home
Close this mind dull this brain Messiah before his fall
What you see is not real Those who know will not tell

Iron Maiden, *Brave New World*, EMI Records Ltd. 2000

Solutions (Worksheet 15)

Brave New World

Dying Swans twisted wings
Beauty not needed here
Lost my love, lost my life
In this garden of fear
I have seen many things
In a lifetime alone
Mother love is no more
Bring this savage back home

Wilderness house of pain
Makes no sense of it all
Close this mind dull this brain
Messiah before his fall
What you see is not real
Those who know will not tell
All is lost sold your soul
To this brave new world

A brave new world
In a brave new world
A brave new world
In a brave new world

Dragon Kings Dying Queens
Where is salvation now
Lost my life lost my dreams
Rip the bones from my flesh
Silent screams laughing here
Dying to tell you the truth
You are planned and you are damned
In this brave new world

A brave new world
In a brave new world
A brave new world
In a brave new world

Iron Maiden, *Brave New World*, EMI Records Ltd. 2000

Weiterführende Materialien

Internetadressen
www.somaweb.org (Links zu allen Aspekten von *Brave* New *World.)*
www. huxley.net/
www.novelguide.com/bravenewworld/
www.webenglishteacher.com/huxley.html (lesson plans)
http://www.sdcoe.kl12.ca/us/score/bnw/bnwtg.html (A Teacher Cyber Guide)
www.readinggroupguide.com/guides/brave_new_world
www.teachers.net/lessons/posts/2161.html

Filme zu den Themen Utopia und Medien
- *Blueprint.* Rolf Schübel. D 2003
- *Brave New World.* (TV) Leslie Libman, Larry Williams. USA 1998
- *Equilibrium.* Kurt Wimmer. USA 2002
- *Gattaca.* Andrew Niccol. USA 1997
- *Pleasantville.* Gary Ross. USA 1998
- *The Fifih Element.* Luc Besson. USA 1997
- *The Matrix.* Andy and Larry Wachowski. USA 1999
- *The Truman Show.* Peter Weir. USA 1998
- *12 Monkeys.* Terry Gilliam. USA 1995

Sachbücher
- Huxley, Aldous: *Brave New World Revisited.* London: 1959
- Postman, Neil: *Amusing Ourselves to Death. Public Discourse in the Age of Show Business.* New York: Penguin 1985

Romane zum Thema Utopia
- Atwood, Margaret: *The Handmaid's Tale.* 1985
- Bellamy, Edward: *Looking Backward: 2000–1887.* 1888
- Bradbury, Ray: *Fahrenheit 451.* 1953
- Burgess, Anthony: *A Clockwork Orange.* 1962
- Orwell, George: *1984.* 1949.
- Morris, William: *News From Nowhere.* 1890
- Wells, H. G.: *Men Like Gods.* 1923
- ders.: *The Time Machine.* 1927
- Zamyatin, Yevgeny: *We.* 1920

Textsammlungen
- Henss, H. (Hrsg.): *Utopian Literature. Texte.* Berlin: Cornelsen 1982
- Ders.: *Utopian Literature. Unterrichtsmodell.* Frankfurt: Hirschgraben 1982.
- Speight, Stephen (Hrsg.): *Discover... The Fascination and Risks of Technology. Students' Book.* Paderborn: Schöningh 2000.
- Ders.: *Discover... The Fascination and Risks of Technology. Teachers' Book.* Paderborn: Schöningh 2001
- Kaußen, Herbert/Renné, Rudi: *Materialienhandbuch Englisch Bd. 2: Mass Media.* Köln: Aulis 1995
- Dies.: *Materialienhandbuch Englisch Bd. 4. Science and Technology.* Köln: Aulis 1997

Musik
Iron Maiden: *Brave New World.* EMI Records Ltd. 2000

Lehrerhandreichungen
- Imig, Ulrich: *Brave New World. Lehrerhandreichungen. Longman Study Texts.* München: Langenscheidt-Longman 1990
- Sonnhütter, Ingrid: *Stundenblätter Aldous Huxley. Brave New World.* Stuttgart: Klett 1983